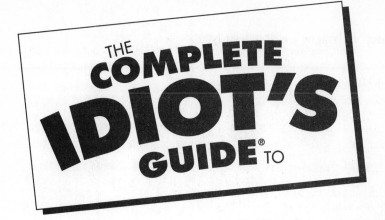

THE **COMPLETE IDIOT'S GUIDE®** TO

Life as a
Military Spouse

D0958732

by Lissa McGrath

ALPHA

A member of Penguin Group (USA) Inc.

This book is dedicated to all the military spouses, new and old, who live the military life standing firmly beside our military men and women. I'm proud to stand alongside you.

ALPHA BOOKS

Published by the Penguin Group

Penguin Group (USA) Inc., 375 Hudson Street, New York, New York 10014, USA

Penguin Group (Canada), 90 Eglinton Avenue East, Suite 700, Toronto, Ontario M4P 2Y3, Canada (a division of Pearson Penguin Canada Inc.)

Penguin Books Ltd., 80 Strand, London WC2R 0RL, England

Penguin Ireland, 25 St. Stephen's Green, Dublin 2, Ireland (a division of Penguin Books Ltd.)

Penguin Group (Australia), 250 Camberwell Road, Camberwell, Victoria 3124, Australia (a division of Pearson Australia Group Pty. Ltd.)

Penguin Books India Pvt. Ltd., 11 Community Centre, Panchsheel Park, New Delhi—110 017, India

Penguin Group (NZ), 67 Apollo Drive, Rosedale, North Shore, Auckland 1311, New Zealand (a division of Pearson New Zealand Ltd.)

Penguin Books (South Africa) (Pty.) Ltd., 24 Sturdee Avenue, Rosebank, Johannesburg 2196, South Africa

Penguin Books Ltd., Registered Offices: 80 Strand, London WC2R 0RL, England

Copyright © 2008 by Lissa McGrath

International Standard Book Number: 978-1-59257-787-3
Library of Congress Catalog Card Number: 2008922781

10   09   08   8   7   6   5   4   3   2   1

Interpretation of the printing code: The rightmost number of the first series of numbers is the year of the book's printing; the rightmost number of the second series of numbers is the number of the book's printing. For example, a printing code of 08-1 shows that the first printing occurred in 2008.

Printed in the United States of America

Note: This publication contains the opinions and ideas of its author. It is intended to provide helpful and informative material on the subject matter covered. It is sold with the understanding that the author and publisher are not engaged in rendering professional services in the book. If the reader requires personal assistance or advice, a competent professional should be consulted.

The author and publisher specifically disclaim any responsibility for any liability, loss, or risk, personal or otherwise, which is incurred as a consequence, directly or indirectly, of the use and application of any of the contents of this book.

Publisher: *Marie Butler-Knight*
Editorial Director: *Mike Sanders*
Senior Managing Editor: *Billy Fields*
Acquisitions Editor: *Tom Stevens*
Development Editor: *Nancy D. Lewis*
Production Editor: *Megan Douglass*
Copy Editor: *Jan Zoya*

Cartoonist: *Steve Barr*
Cover Designer: *Becky Harmon*
Book Designer: *Trina Wurst*
Indexer: *Celia McCoy*
Layout: *Ayanna Lacey*
Proofreader: *Laura Caddell*

Contents at a Glance

Contents

Introduction

I'm sure you've heard the phrase "The only thing harder than being a Soldier is loving one." Feel free to substitute Sailor, Marine, Airman, Coastie, reservist, or Guard member in here. It fits for all branches. Being a military spouse can be tough.

You're responsible for taking care of the family when your spouse is gone, you're the listening ear when your spouse needs it, you're a mechanic, handyman, daycare provider, chef, and may hold a full-time job as well. And you are expected to do all of this with a calm, personable demeanor. Yes, being a military spouse is tough, but it's also incredibly rewarding. Personally, I wouldn't trade this life for anything.

The point of this book is to make your life as a military spouse a little easier. This book will give you the tools to make the most of the benefits available to you, as well as show you some little-known programs and resources that can make things a lot easier.

If you're new to the military, then I'm sure you have hundreds of questions and don't really know where to start. Well, you've come to the right place. Whether you're the fiancée of a servicemember, and brand new to the military world, or you're a seasoned spouse with multiple deployments under your belt, you will find something here to make your life easier.

This book is about empowerment through knowledge. If you know the resources, programs, and benefits available to you, then you can be proactive about making your own life easier. The information in this book covers all active-duty branches as well as National Guard, reserve, and retirees. So I hope no one feels left out!

You'll notice I write from a female point of view. If you're a male spouse, please do not be offended. I chose to write from a female perspective because 90 percent of military spouses are female. However, I do address issues specifically for male spouses, and all the programs and resources I reference in this book also apply to you.

How this book is organized:

Part 1, "Family and Finances," shows you how to become an "official" military spouse. It covers challenges such as getting married when time is limited, or your fiancé is deployed, and what to do if you're a foreign-born citizen (including the immigration options open to you). It shows the financial benefits to being a military family, from shopping, to pay and allowances, education, health care, and more. It also shows you what to expect if you decide to have children and the care you can expect at a military hospital. Here we also cover the support and programs available to you through your Family Support Center.

Part 2, "Moving in the Military," tackles the issues you face during a move, from planning and preparing the kids, to actually moving and then settling in, as well as finding a new home and a new job. We even show you what to expect during a move overseas.

Part 3, "Help, My Spouse Is Getting Deployed," guides you through this most challenging of times. We cover the full deployment cycle and what to expect emotionally for yourself, your spouse, and your kids. We look at ways to help you and your family cope during the deployment, whether it's five months or fifteen. It's hard to think about, but we also cover what happens if your spouse is injured, or worse. The final chapter helps you plan for your spouse's retirement from the military, and explains what benefits you will retain.

Extras

Throughout this book you will find tips and suggestions that I've discovered for myself or have learned from other spouses. This is invaluable information that you usually only get by word-of-mouth, and often too late for it to be helpful for the task at hand.

Ask the Chief
In this type of sidebar you'll find more information that will give you a better understanding of the topic at hand, or might just be interesting to know.

def•i•ni•tion
The military has more acronyms than I've seen anywhere else. Here I will define not only the common acronyms but what they, and other military terms, actually mean.

Top's Tips

Here you will find tips to make your life easier and help you maximize benefits and resources available to you.

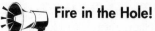

Fire in the Hole!

Don't ignore these side-bars. These are cautions to help prevent you from doing something wrong that could lose you money, or worse.

From Seasoned Spouses

Seasoned spouses have been around a while and have truly been there, done that. The anecdotes you'll find here are from my own experience and those of other spouses. They should help put things into perspective and show you how things work in the military world.

Acknowledgments

As always, a huge thank-you goes out to Tom Stevens, Nancy Lewis, Megan Douglass, and the entire team at Alpha. You guys are the best! And also to my agent, Marilyn Allen, thank you for your support and expertise.

I would also like to thank my husband, Chris, for his love and support. Even though you're far away right now, your support and encouragement stays with me every day. We can't wait for you to come home!

And finally, I would like to thank each and every military spouse who shared their experiences to help me write this book. This book would not have been nearly as good without your input.

Special Thanks to the Technical Editors

The Complete Idiot's Guide to Life as a Military Spouse was reviewed by military spouses from multiple branches of the military to ensure the programs I've discussed and terminology used is accurate for all branches. Special thanks are extended to Heather Flow (National Guard spouse), Schaele Dodson (Army spouse), and Melody Webb (retired active-duty Navy and spouse of a Command Master Chief).

Trademarks

All terms mentioned in this book that are known to be or are suspected of being trademarks or service marks have been appropriately capitalized. Alpha Books and Penguin Group (USA) Inc. cannot attest to the accuracy of this information. Use of a term in this book should not be regarded as affecting the validity of any trademark or service mark.

Part 1

Family and Finances

Getting started in the military can be daunting, and if you're originally from another country, it's even more challenging. This first part will take you through the steps to becoming a recognized military spouse (including immigration if needed), the financial benefits that are now available to you and your family, how to create a budget, the family support services open to you, and what to expect when and if you decide to have a child while your spouse is in the military.

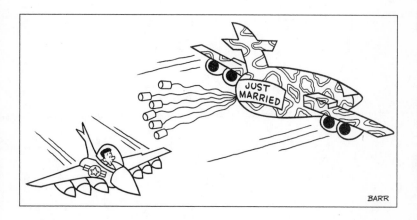

Marrying Into the Military

In This Chapter

- ◆ Becoming an "official" military spouse
- ◆ Picking your TRICARE policy
- ◆ Immigration challenges for foreign-born spouses
- ◆ Which is better, a fiancée visa or spouse visa?
- ◆ How to get married when they (or you) can't be there

Joining the military community can be a bit daunting, particularly because there are quite a few hoops you have to jump through after you get married, before the military considers you an official spouse (or "dependent" as you will be forever known by the military).

This chapter will help you navigate getting through all of the paperwork. It also covers what to do if, like me, you weren't born in the United States. We're going to cover what you should do before you get married, and also how immigration works if you got married in your home country.

For now, though, we'll start with the basics that all new military spouses face: getting registered as a new family member.

Getting an ID Card

Getting your military ID card is the first step to being recognized as part of your spouse's family. If your spouse is with you, it's really easy. He will make an appointment (some bases also have walk-in service), and you both go in with a certified copy of your marriage certificate (not the display one you got at the wedding) to prove you are married.

Your spouse will fill out a form that registers you in *DEERS*.

def•i•ni•tion

DEERS (Defense Enrollment Eligibility Reporting System) is a database of all military personnel and their dependents. Until you are enrolled in DEERS, you cannot use any military services or benefits.

The form for DEERS registration and getting an ID card is the same. If you have children from a previous marriage in your custody, then the child will be eligible for military services, including health care. Your spouse will need to register every child with DEERS, but only children over 10 years old actually need an ID card.

Military ID cards look different depending on who they are for. As a dependent of an active-duty member, you will get a brown laminated card. Retirees have cards that look identical to yours except they are green.

Throughout this book you'll hear me use two words very frequently: *sponsor* and *dependent*. The "sponsor" is the military member. "Dependent" refers to any member of his family who is dependent on him.

Now, I know many military spouses earn far more than their active-duty counterpart, but you are still considered a dependent by the military, as are any children you have together. Step-children can also be registered as dependents.

To find your closest ID card office, go to www.dmdc.osd.mil/rsl/owa/home. You can search by city, state, zip code, base name, or country.

Make sure to call and see if you need an appointment (phone numbers are part of the results).

TRICARE

Once you are registered in DEERS you can register for TRICARE, which is the military's health-care insurance. Go to your local military treatment facility (MTF), which is usually a military hospital on-base or close by, and visit the TRICARE office. You can register online if you are not close to a MTF.

There are various types of TRICARE coverage, which depend on a variety of factors such as whether you are active-duty, reserve, or retired, or living overseas or at a remote location, etc.

I could write an entire book about TRICARE, but there's just not the space here. Thankfully, TRICARE makes it easy to see what plans you should be eligible for, and even lets you compare different plans.

Go to www.tricare.mil/mybenefit/home/overview/PlanWizard.jsp to use the Plan Wizard to determine which plans you may be eligible for. Click Compare Plans in the gray bar beneath the main tabs on the page (or go directly to www.tricare.mil/mybenefit/home/overview/ ComparePlans).

TRICARE Plans

You can get all the details about these plans from www.tricare.mil, but here are the basics:

TRICARE Prime   The most common plan for active-duty members and their dependents living in the United States. Any treatment or appointments will be at the local military hospital unless they do not have the facility/specialists needed. If that's the case, you will be referred to a civilian provider and a per-visit co-pay will apply for dependents (usually $12 per visit).

TRICARE Standard and Extra   This is the plan for active-duty dependents who prefer to see a civilian provider for all care. It is a fee-for-service plan, so you don't pay a monthly premium, but this does have the highest out-of-pocket cost for dependents. TRICARE Extra is cheaper, and is used when the doctor is an in-network provider.

TRICARE Prime Remote   For active-duty members and their dependents who live farther than 50 miles or one hour's drive from the nearest military treatment facility. You will be assigned a civilian in-network Primary Care Manager (PCM). This provider will give referrals for specialty care as a PCM in TRICARE Prime would.

TRICARE Reserve Select   This is for reservists, National Guard members, and their dependents when they are not activated for over 30 days. The coverage is very similar to TRICARE Standard, but there is a monthly premium to pay. For just the member it is $81 per month. To cover the whole family, it is $253 per month. The annual deductible is $50 for individual and $100 for family if the member's rank is E4 or below. For E5 and above it is $150 for individual and $300 for family. The cost to you (after deductible) is approximately 15 percent for most services.

TRICARE For Life   TRICARE beneficiaries entitled to Medicare Part A and who have purchased Medicare Part B are also entitled to coverage from TRICARE. Medicare pays first when both plans cover the treatment. The deductibles are the same as for TRICARE Reserve Select.

Ask the Chief

Reservists, National Guard members, and their dependents are eligible for TRICARE Prime, TRICARE Standard and Extra, and TRICARE Prime Remote, if they are activated for over 30 consecutive days. If you marry a retired service-member, you are also entitled to TRICARE coverage.

If you are overseas, there are versions of all of these plans for you. They are TRICARE Prime Overseas, TRICARE Standard Overseas (there is no TRICARE Extra because there are no in-network providers), TRICARE Global Remote Overseas, and TRICARE Reserve Select While Overseas. The coverage is pretty much the same, but we'll cover this more in Chapter 10.

TRICARE Regions

The United States is divided into regions, each with a specific provider who handles all of the claims, services, etc. for that area. When you move, you may well change regions.

TRICARE North—Connecticut, Delaware, District of Columbia, Illinois, Indiana, Kentucky, Maine, Maryland, Massachusetts, Michigan, New Hampshire, New Jersey, New York, North Carolina, Ohio, Pennsylvania, Rhode Island, Vermont, Virginia, West Virginia, Wisconsin, and portions of Iowa (Rock Island Arsenal area), Missouri (St. Louis area), and Tennessee (Ft. Campbell area).

TRICARE South—Alabama, Arkansas, Florida, Georgia, Louisiana, Mississippi, Oklahoma, South Carolina, Tennessee (excluding the Ft. Campbell area), and Texas (excluding the El Paso area).

TRICARE West—Alaska, Arizona, California, Colorado, Hawaii, Idaho, Iowa (excluding Rock Island Arsenal area), Kansas, Minnesota, Missouri (except the St. Louis area), Montana, Nebraska, Nevada, New Mexico, North Dakota, Oregon, South Dakota, Texas (the southwestern corner, including El Paso), Utah, Washington, and Wyoming.

Contact Information for Each TRICARE Region

TRICARE Region	Provider	Phone Number	Website
North	HealthNet	1-877-874-2273	www.healthnetfederalservices.com
South	Humana Military	1-800-444-5445	www.humana-military.com
West	TriWest	1-888-874-9378	www.triwest.com

The information for overseas TRICARE Area Offices (TAO) can be found in Chapter 10 with other overseas specific information.

When you first enroll with TRICARE you have the choice to request a Primary Care Manager (PCM). It's worth asking around and finding out who is a good person to see so you can request that person. If you don't put anything down, any provider (of the gender you select) will be assigned. You can request a PCM change later, but it's better to do your research first.

When you call to make an appointment, you will be asked for your sponsor's Social Security number (SSN). Get used to this. You won't need your own SSN for anything to do with the military. Whenever you go to an appointment, bring your ID card with you. This shows you are eligible for the services provided. You will also get a TRICARE insurance card, which you'll need if you are seen by a civilian, in an Emergency Room, or any treatment facility other than your usual one. Children under 10 don't usually have ID cards, so you will use yours when you take your child to an on-base medical appointment. However, they do get TRICARE insurance cards, so keep that safe for off-base referrals.

Immigration Challenges

If you are not a U.S. resident, getting married takes a bit more planning than just getting a marriage license. Whether you are married in your home country or in the United States, you are going to need a visa to enter the United States to be with your new spouse.

Before I go any further, I need to reiterate that I am not a lawyer, let alone an immigration lawyer, so please take this as advice from someone who's been there, done that, but nothing more. You should always contact your immigration office if you have any questions or concerns. The United States Citizenship and Immigration Service (USCIS) has a website with a wealth of information including current processing times, updated forms, costs, etc. I strongly recommend you check it out. They even have a military specific page at www.uscis.gov/military and a phone number strictly for military families at 1-877-247-4645.

Two visa petitions that can be used to get you Permanent Resident status: fiancée (I-129F) and spouse (I-130).

If you are already married, you must file a spouse visa petition (I-130), which costs $355. You will not be able to enter the United States until it is approved (which could be seven months or more), but once you get here you are automatically a Permanent Resident and legally allowed to work.

If you are not already married, and your fiancé is a U.S. citizen stationed stateside, you may prefer the fiancée visa (I-129F) option. This is more expensive in the long run because there are more hoops to jump through, but the advantage is you are with your spouse in the United States while the majority of the processing is done. The processing time is usually around four months and costs $455.

You have four months from when the petition is approved to enter the United States, then 90 days to get married once you arrive. After that, you will need to file for Adjustment of Status (I-485) to become a Permanent Resident. The $1,010 Adjustment of Status fee includes the filing fees for employment authorization (I-765) and a travel document (I-131) to allow you to travel out of the country while it's processing. The Adjustment Of Status petition currently takes about seven months (the employment authorization and travel document take less time).

The on-base legal office can show your fiancé/spouse which forms are needed for each petition and how to complete them.

You may become a Conditional Permanent Resident for two years under two circumstances: You enter on a fiancée visa, or you enter on a spouse visa but you were married for less than two years when the visa was approved.

If either of these apply to you, you will have to file another form (I-751) two years after you receive your Permanent Resident Card (green card) to remove the conditions. This costs $545.

The total cost to get you to a 10 year Permanent Resident Card via the fiancée visa route is $2,010. For a spouse visa it is $355 if you've been married over two years when you file, or $900 if it's less than two years.

Obviously, $900 is a lot less than $2,010, but it will involve your being separated from your spouse after you are already married. If this separation isn't a problem for you (e.g., he's deployed, or you have college to finish, etc.) then this is probably a better option, but check the current processing times for your service center (at https://egov.uscis.gov/cris/jsps/ptimes.jsp) before deciding.

Military Expedite

There are certain circumstances where visa petitions can be expedited. There are many emergent situations on the list, but one of them is military deployment.

If you have already filed an application, your fiancé should call the military helpline (1-877-247-4645) and let them know that he would like to put an "expedite request" on the petition on grounds of military deployment. He will have to fax a copy of his military ID and deployment orders and/or a letter from his command stating when he will be deployed. If the expedite is approved, you will know the outcome of the petition request within five days (approved or denied).

If you're filing a fiancée visa petition, you still have to meet with your local American Consulate and fulfill the medical requirements, but this could drastically reduce the wait time.

If you have not already filed the petition, the evidence of military service and deployment and a letter requesting the expedite should be included in the petition packet and sent via Express Mail to the appropriate service center.

If you have any questions on how to do this, contact your on-base legal office, or call the USCIS helpline at 1-877-247-4645.

What if My Fiancé Isn't a U.S. Citizen?

Although there is a fast-track process for United States military service-members to become U.S. citizens, not all choose to take advantage of this.

If this is the case for you, and your spouse is a U.S. Permanent Resident, not a citizen, he can still file for a spouse visa on your behalf. In fact, this is the only option you have, because he cannot file for a fiancée visa.

The processing time for an I-130 petition filed by a Permanent Resident is much longer than if a U.S. citizen files it. Currently, the waiting time is two or three years depending on which service center is processing your application.

Honestly, naturalization to become a citizen takes a lot less time than that. So, if your fiancé intends to become a citizen anyway, it is probably better to wait for him to have his N-400 petition approved (which is free for most active-duty and ready-reserve) and then file either the fiancée or spouse visa at that point.

If your spouse's N-400 takes seven months, and your visa takes six months, that's still only thirteen months total. That's far better than two to three years.

For more information about your spouse becoming a citizen, read the Naturalization Information for Military Personnel guide at www.uscis. gov/files/article/MilitaryBrochurev7.pdf.

Becoming a Citizen

You do not have to become a citizen. You can apply for a reentry permit if you are stationed overseas and retain your permanent residency if you prefer. However, there are a couple of perks to being military during this process.

If you are married to a U.S. citizen in the military, you only need to have three years of residency in the United States (as opposed to the general five years) before applying for citizenship. But it gets better. If you take orders overseas, that waiting period disappears.

So if you get your green card, and two months later your spouse is transferred overseas on an accompanied tour (for over one year), you can immediately file your N-400 petition (it costs $675 if you're not active-duty or former military). You can read more about this at www. uscis.gov/files/article/M-476.pdf.

Visa Don'ts

Don't enter the United States on a tourist visa (or any other type of nonimmigrant visa), get married, and stay here. You will have a much harder time adjusting your status to permanent resident, and it might be denied outright. Plus, you'll have to pay an extra $1,000 as a fine for doing it "the wrong way."

Don't leave the United States while your I-485 is in processing unless you have already received your travel authorization document and reentry permit. You'll have little trouble leaving, but you won't be able to reenter the United States.

Can I Work?

When you enter the United States on a fiancée visa, your airport immigration officer may stamp your passport "work authorized." That gives you the ability to work while you're in the country on your nonimmigrant visa. I was able to get this from Seattle airport when I entered in June 2001, but that was before 9/11 and I haven't been given a straight answer about whether this is still allowed or not.

> **Top's Tips**
>
> Even if your passport is stamped, you will still need to file the I-765, because your work authorization expires once your fiancée visa expires (90 days from entry to the United States).

If your passport is not stamped work authorized, then you cannot work. You'll need to wait until you file your I-485 and file the I-765 Application for Employment Authorization at the same time. There is no additional fee for this.

Should I Get a Lawyer?

You already have one! Military legal offices offer many services, one of them is immigration assistance. Your spouse can make an appointment with the attorney who will help him decide which visa is most appropriate for your situation, and assist him with the paperwork. The best part is it's all free!

If your spouse is in the Reserves or National Guard, you can still receive free assistance, just not from military lawyers. Go to www.uscis.gov/legaladvice and click on Free Legal Service Providers. Select your spouse's state and it will show you free legal providers in that area who specialize in immigration help.

If after talking to a free provider (or military legal) you still think you need an "immigration" lawyer, then they should be able to point you in the right direction.

What If My Spouse Is Deployed for My Green Card Interview?

This happened to me. You'll get your appointment date a few months in advance. If you know your spouse will be deployed, the first thing to do is contact the immigration office and let them know the situation. Do this by mail and make sure your letter is sent via certified mail so there is a signature card returned to you proving it was delivered and who signed for it.

You will need a copy of your spouse's orders, and a letter from the command showing that he is deployed. I ended up having to get my Congressman's office involved to get an answer on whether or not they would interview me without my spouse.

If you do have to get the Congressperson's office involved, make sure to ask who the head of the Adjustment of Status department is. It can make a big difference, being able to ask to speak to that person by name if you do have issues when you get to your interview. I was able to be interviewed without my spouse, but other field offices may have different rules.

Top's Tips

There is someone at every Congressperson's office who deals with immigration issues. They have a contact person at the CIS whose job it is to answer the Congressperson's office queries.

Proxy Marriage—When He Can't Be There in Person

One challenge that faces many fiancées is that their spouse-to-be is deployed, going deployed on short notice, stationed overseas, etc. This is where *proxy marriages* can help.

def•i•ni•tion

A **proxy marriage** is when there is a stand-in for the bride or groom because one person or the other couldn't be physically present at the ceremony.

Proxy marriages are only legally obtained in a handful of states, but all U.S. states recognize them as legal. Single-proxy (when one person is not able to be there) is legal under any conditions in Colorado, Montana, and Texas. A single-proxy marriage is also legal in California, but only if you are a California resident and your fiancé is deployed.

In Montana, a double-proxy marriage is legal. This is when neither the bride nor groom is physically present. So, if you are in need of a proxy marriage but don't live in one of the legal states, you can have a double-proxy marriage arranged for you in Montana (expect to pay about $900).

The Least You Need to Know

◆ Getting registered in DEERS makes you an officially recognized military spouse (dependent).

◆ There's a TRICARE policy for pretty much every military person in any location worldwide.

◆ From now on you will need your spouse's Social Security number for everything to do with the military (including scheduling medical appointments).

◆ Fiancée visas can only be filed by U.S. citizens, and require you to be married in the United States. Spouse visas are cheaper, but you must be outside of the United States while it is processed.

◆ The U.S. Citizenship and Immigration Service has a helpline for military families at 1-877-247-4645.

◆ Legal offices on-base can help you with your immigration paperwork.

Chapter 2

Understanding Pay and Allowances

In This Chapter

- ◆ How much your spouse really makes
- ◆ Special pay and tax-free allowances
- ◆ Reenlistment bonuses
- ◆ Creating a realistic budget and reducing debt
- ◆ How to read an LES

Not all military benefits are financial, however this is a good place to start. In this chapter, we're going to look at the types of pay your spouse may receive, as well as clarify job-specific and location-specific pays that might be applicable to you.

Basic Pays

All basic pays (for active-duty) are the same, no matter what branch of military your spouse is in. These all show up on your spouse's *LES*. Some are taxable; some are not.

def•i•ni•tion

LES stands for Leave and Earning Statement. This is your spouse's pay-stub. He can get it online through his MyPay account (https://mypay.dfas.mil). We will cover how to read an LES later in this chapter.

Military Pay Tables

This is the main "income" portion for your spouse. This is taxable (unless your spouse is in a hazard duty zone).

These tables are for 2008. Each year (around early November) the rates for the following year are signed into law. This year the raise was 3.5 percent, but it varies from year to year. The highest I've seen was 11 percent, and the lowest was 2 percent.

Pay Grade	<2	2	3	4	6	8	10	12	14	16	18	20	22	24	26
E9	-	-	-	-	-	-	4255	4351	4472	4616	4759	4991	5186	5392	5706
E8	-	-	-	-	3483	3637	3732	3847	3970	4194	4307	4499	4606	4870
E7	2421	2642	2744	2878	2982	3162	3263	3443	3593	3695	3803	3845	3987	4063	4351
E6	2094	2304	2406	2504	2608	2840	2930	3105	3159	3198	3243	3243	3243	3243	3243
E5	1919	2047	2146	2247	2405	2571	2705	2722	2722	2722	2722	2722	2722	2722	2722
E4	1759	1849	1949	2048	2135	2135	2135	2135	2135	2135	2135	2135	2135	2135	2135
E3	1588	1688	1790	1790	1790	1790	1790	1790	1790	1790	1790	1790	1790	1790	1790
E2	1510	1510	1510	1510	1510	1510	1510	1510	1510	1510	1510	1510	1510	1510	1510
E1	1347	1347	1347	1347	1347	1347	1347	1347	1347	1347	1347	1347	1347	1347	1347

Footnote: E1 with less than 4 months is $1245.90

Enlisted Monthly Basic Pay Effective January 1, 2008.

Pay Grade	<2	2	3	4	6	8	10	12	14	16	18	20	22	24	26
O10	-	-	-	-	-	-	-	-	-	-	-	14137	14206	14502	15017
O9	-	-	-	-	-	-	-	-	-	-	-	12365	12543	12800	13249
O8	8749	9035	9226	9279	9516	9912	10005	10381	10489	10814	11282	11715	12004	12004	12004
O7	7270	7607	7764	7888	8113	8335	8592	8848	9105	9912	10594	10594	10594	10594	10648
O6	5388	5919	6308	6308	6332	6603	6639	6639	7016	7684	8075	8466	8689	8915	9352
O5	4492	5060	5411	5476	5695	5826	6113	6324	6596	7014	7212	7409	7631	7631	7631
O4	3876	4487	4786	4853	5130	5428	5799	6088	6289	6404	6471	6471	6471	6471	6471
O3	3407	3863	4169	4546	4763	5002	5157	5411	5543	5543	5543	5543	5543	5543	5543
O2	2944	3353	3862	3992	4074	4074	4074	4074	4074	4074	4074	4074	4074	4074	4074
O1	2556	2660	3215	3215	3215	3215	3215	3215	3215	3215	3215	3215	3215	3215	3215
Commissioned Officers with more than four years as enlisted or warrant officers:															
O3E	-	-	-	4546	4763	5002	5157	5411	5626	5749	5916	5916	5916	5916	5916
O2E	-	-	-	3992	4074	4204	4423	4592	4718	4718	4718	4718	4718	4718	4718
O1E	-	-	-	3215	3434	3560	3690	3818	3992	3992	3992	3992	3992	3992	3992

Officer Monthly Basic Pay Effective January 1, 2008.

Pay Grade	<2	2	3	4	6	8	10	12	14	16	18	20	22	24	26
W5	-	-	-	-	-	-	-	-	-	-	-	6261	6579	6815	7078
W4	3521	3788	3897	4004	4188	4370	4555	4833	5076	5308	5497	5682	5954	6176	6431
W3	3125	3350	3487	3532	3676	3960	4255	4403	4554	4720	5018	5219	5339	5467	5641
W2	2846	3115	3197	3255	3439	3726	3868	4008	4179	4313	4434	4579	4674	4750	4750
W1	2498	2766	2839	2992	3163	3439	3563	3737	3908	4042	4166	4316	4316	4316	4316

Warrant Officer Monthly Basic Pay Effective January 1, 2008.

For space reasons, I have rounded figures in these tables to the nearest whole dollar. To see the current pay charts go to www.dfas.mil/militarypay.html, click on Military Pay Tables, and then select the current year.

Reservists and National Guard are paid Drill Pay for their service and training when not activated. The tables are too big to print here. Go to www.dfas.mil/militarypay.html, click Military Pay Tables, and then select the current year. The pay tables are on page 9 of the PDF that opens. One drill period is four hours and a typical weekend is four drill periods.

How Incentive Pay Works

If you only look at the basic pay table it looks like your spouse doesn't earn very much. But as your spouse becomes qualified in different skills, you will start to notice additional incentive pays which can really add up.

The following table lists some of the main incentive pays. You can view all of the tables for incentive pays at www.dfas.mil/militarypay.html.

Incentive Pay (Monthly)

Type of Pay	Amount
Aviation Career Incentive Pay	$125–$840
Hazardous Duty Incentive Pay (HDIP*) Crew Member	$150–$250
HDIP* Noncrew Member	$150
Imminent Danger Pay/Hostile Fire Pay	$225
Diving Pay (officer)	max. $240

continues

Incentive Pay (Monthly) (continued)

Type of Pay	Amount
Diving Pay (enlisted)	max. $340
Submarine Duty Incentive Pay	$75–$835
Career Sea Pay (Navy/Marine Corps)	$50–700
Career Sea Pay (Army)	$50–646
Career Sea Pay (Air Force)	$50–520

HDIP is more commonly called Flight Pay, which makes the "crew member" and "noncrew member" make a lot more sense.

Where there is an amount range, it is usually based on the number of years serving in that capacity, or the qualification level of the service-member. Where cumulative years of service are a factor, only time actually serving in that capacity count. So, for career sea pay, only the time at a sea billet counts. If your spouse is assigned to a shore command, this time in service doesn't count toward the career sea pay cumulative total.

Your spouse may be entitled to Hardship Duty Pay (HDP) because of a specific mission, or a location he is stationed at (or deployed to for over 30 days). For example, the HDP for Iraq, Afghanistan, or Kuwait right now is $100 a month. But it's not just hostile areas. Greenland has a HDP of $150 a month, Poland is $50 a month, and those in the Philippines get $100 a month.

Officers in medical fields are given incentives for continuing to serve in the military. The amount is based on qualifications and time in service. Some are paid monthly, others are yearly bonuses. They range from $100 a month to $36,000 per year.

What Is an SRB and Who Is Eligible?

An SRB, or Selective Reenlistment Bonus, is a monetary incentive to get enlisted personnel into undermanned jobs, or to get those in highly specialized fields to reenlist. Officers are not eligible for SRBs.

The theory is that it is cheaper to give a bonus to someone who is already trained and experienced than to start from scratch with someone new. Not all servicemembers are eligible for SRBs, and the amount varies considerably based on their *MOS/NEC.*

def•i•ni•tion

MOS stands for Military Occupational Specialty. It is the job that your spouse does in the military. In the Navy this is referred to as your **NEC** (Navy Enlisted Classification).

The SRB could be $2,000, or $90,000. It also depends on whether the reenlistment is Zone A, B, or C.

◆ Zone A: 2 to 6 years in service

◆ Zone B: 6 years 1 day, to 10 years in service

◆ Zone C: 10 years 1 day, to 14 years in service

For example, when my husband first reenlisted, he was an E4 with four years of service. He reenlisted for six years and received $32,000 for his Zone A reenlistment bonus. He just reenlisted again in 2007 as an E7 with 10 years in service (he reenlisted on his 10-year enlistment anniversary so he was still eligible for Zone B). The bonus was lower because it was Zone B, and his NEC is not as critically manned as it used to be. Still, he received $16,000, which was a nice bonus. His NEC is not eligible for a Zone C bonus, so this is the last one he gets.

In the Navy, you receive half of the SRB amount when your spouse reenlists and the rest is split into equal installments and paid each year in the month of his reenlistment until the term is up. All other branches give the full SRB amount at the time of reenlistment, rather than in installments.

Top's Tips

If your spouse reenlists while in a hazard duty zone (stationed there or deployed), his SRB becomes completely tax-free. That's 25 percent extra in your pocket. So, if your spouse is eligible for an SRB and close to deployment, he should talk to his career counselor about the options available.

Very few MOS/NECs offer SRBs for servicemembers over 14 years. By 14 years you've only got 6 more years before you'll get retirement benefits. The military considers that enough incentive to stay in for one more term (they're usually right).

Allowances and How They Differ from Pay

The difference between a "pay" and an "allowance" is that a pay is taxable (unless your spouse is in a designated combat zone) and an allowance is always nontaxable.

The two allowances all families are eligible for are Basic Allowance for Subsistence (BAS—your food) and Basic Allowance for Housing (BAH—your home). The BAS rates for 2008 are $294.43 a month for enlisted servicemembers (all branches and pay grades), and $202.76 for all officers.

Your BAH rate is based on the housing costs of where you live. There are many different types of BAH, which apply during different situations.

BAH for Active-Duty Families

If your spouse is active-duty, the only two that really concern you are *BAH with dependents* and *BAH without dependents*.

Once you are entered into DEERS, your spouse will start getting BAH with dependents. This can be quite a large jump. For example, the 2008 BAH for an E4 at McChord Air Force Base is $901 for without dependents, and $1201 for with dependents. The difference for officers is about the same. An O3 without dependents gets $1,421, and with dependents he gets $1,773.

You only need one bedroom whether you're single or married without children. So the BAH jump from without dependents to with dependents means you can get a nicer place than your spouse could afford when he was single. Alternatively, if you stay at his (or your) current place, you get a few hundred dollars extra to go toward utilities or just to pocket. Unfortunately, the BAH rate does not increase if you have more than one dependent.

Here's how to find the BAH rate for any location:

1. Go to http://perdiem.hqda.pentagon.mil.

2. Click BAH on the shortcut menu at the top of the page.

3. Enter your base zip code and your spouse's rank (E3, O2, etc.).

4. Click Execute.

This will show the with dependents and without dependents rates.

BAH rates change yearly based on the local housing rental market, and can go up or down. However Individual Rate Protection assures you will continue getting the higher of the two rates (the old rate he got in December, or the new rate effective in January) until your spouse *PCS*'s, changes status (goes from without dependents to with dependents, or vice versa), or is reduced in rank.

def•i•ni•tion

PCS stands for Permanent Change of Station. This is when you get orders to move to another base.

All new additions to the base after January first will be paid the new rate no matter how it compares to last year's rate.

If you are a dual-military couple, you are both entitled to BAH. If you have no children, you will each receive the without dependents rate. If you have kids, one of you will receive BAH with dependents, and the other will get BAH without dependents.

National Guard and Reservist BAH

If your spouse is activated National Guard or reserve for over 30 days, he is eligible for full BAH. However, if he's activated for less than 30 days, the rate is lower.

This is called Basic Allowance for Housing Reserve Component/ Transit, or BAH (RC/T). The old name (which you'll probably still hear) is BAH Type II (or BAH II). The rates are different for single, partial (no dependents and living in barracks), and with dependents. Because this book deals with families, the rates shown are for with dependents only.

2008 BAH RC/T Rates (Effective Jan 1, 2008)

Pay Grade	Monthly with Dependents Rate
O10	$1,587.30
O9	$1,587.30
O8	$1,587.30
O7	$1,587.30
O6	$1,428.90
O5	$1,377.30
O4	$1,214.10
O3	$1,004.70
O2	$857.10
O1	$767.40
O3E	$1,079.70
O2E	$974.10
O1E	$900.60
W5	$1,172.40
W4	$1,074.60
W3	$984.90
W2	$905.10
W1	$783.30
E9	$1,031.10
E8	$951.30
E7	$882.90
E6	$815.70
E5	$733.80
E4	$637.80
E3	$593.40
E2	$565.50
E1	$565.50

You can see rates for your current year by going to http://perdiem.hqda.pentagon.mil, clicking on BAH, and then on Non-Locality Rates. New rates are usually released mid-December.

Your spouse receives $1/30$ of the rate in the table for each day he is activated. So if your spouse is an E6, he will receive $27.19 for each day he is in activated status ($815.70 ÷ 30 = $27.19). If he's activated for 18 days, he will get $489.42.

Family Separation Allowance (FSA)

If your spouse is deployed, or is on an unaccompanied tour (stationed somewhere that you cannot join him), then you are eligible for the Family Separation Allowance (FSA). This is $250 per month for all pay grades (Officer and Enlisted).

Cost of Living Allowance (COLA)

Many overseas locations have COLA because living expenses there are higher. Some areas within the United States also have it. Overseas it's called O-COLA (OCONUS Cost Of Living Allowance) and within the United States it's called C-COLA (CONUS Cost Of Living Allowance). It is only for nonhousing excessive living expenses.

Go to http://perdiem.hqda.pentagon.mil to see if your area has COLA. Click on C-COLA in the Shortcuts at the top of the page. Enter your base zip code, your spouse's rank and years of service, and select Yes for the dependents option. If your area has COLA, the amount will be displayed. If not, it will say, "Zip code 98438 does not receive COLA for FY08."

You can see a list of the C-COLA locations by clicking the COLA Locations button on the same page.

Clothing Allowance

This is another enlisted-only allowance. Each year in the month your spouse enlisted in the military you will be given a clothing allowance to help with the cost of replacing uniforms.

The allowances are different for each branch and gender because uniform costs vary. The first table shows the initial clothing allowance. This is for your spouse's first sets of uniforms and is higher because he has to buy all of the uniforms at once.

Fiscal Year 2008 Initial Clothing Allowance (Effective October 1, 2007)

Branch	Male	Female
Army	$1,330.70	$1,622.36
Navy	$1,203.64	$1,432.15
Air Force	$1,292.89	$1,499.21
Marine Corps	$1,596.43	$1,879.05
Coast Guard	$1,142.36	$1,244.28

The next table is the yearly replacement allowance you will receive on the anniversary of your spouse's enlistment. The rates can go up or down. 2008's rates are higher for the Navy because a lot of the uniforms changed. The rates are available in the military pay tables at www.dfas.mil/militarypay.html.

Fiscal Year 2008 Replacement Clothing Allowance (Effective October 1, 2007)

Branch	Basic Rate		Standard Rate	
	Male	Female	Male	Female
Army	$370.80	$432.00	$529.20	$619.20
Navy	$464.40	$475.20	$662.40	$680.40
Air Force	$316.80	$349.20	$453.60	$496.80
Marine Corps	$360.00	$385.20	$514.80	$550.80
Coast Guard	$337.78	$346.47	$478.26	$494.97

The basic rate is paid for the first three years of enlistment. It is lower because the uniforms purchased with the initial clothing allowance are expected to last up to three years. The amount is based on how long they estimate it will take for uniforms to wear out.

The Navy pays E7-E9 a higher rate because they have more uniforms and they are more expensive than the uniforms for E6 and below. For 2008, the replacement allowance rates are $871.20 for men and $939.60 for women.

So you can see, when you add in special pays, SRB amounts, and allowances, the amount your spouse actually makes is a lot higher than it initially looks. There are also many other nonpay financial benefits which we will cover in Chapter 3.

Creating a Realistic Budget

Creating a budget is important whether you're an E3 or O3. An O3 may make more money, but it's easy to overextend, whatever your income.

I've heard people say that it's not worth making a budget because family finances change so often, when their spouse deploys, they PCS, etc. Personally, I think it's more important simply because of that. If you keep an electronic copy on your computer, it's very easy to update whenever something changes.

Top's Tips

When your spouse deploys, you make more money than when he is at home. If you stick to the budget as if your spouse is home even when he's gone, you'll have extra money to put into savings or to pay off debt.

Understanding an LES

You'll need to use your spouse's most recent Leave Earning Statement (LES) to get all the income specifics for your budget.

Your spouse can download his LES at http://mypay.dfas.mil. Your spouse may obtain a Restricted Access Pin for you so you can view his LES and tax statement but cannot make changes to his pay specifics. This is particularly useful when he's deployed.

In the situation that your spouse is injured, or a pay issue arises, you will need to know how to read an LES. Thankfully DFAS (the Defense Finance and Accounting Service) provides "how to" information for each type of LES (some branches are different from others). Go to www.dfas.mil/militarypay/newinformation.html and select your spouse's branch of service (reserve and National Guard LES instructions are also provided).

All of the acronyms are explained on the LES itself, and the income and outgoing expenses are clearly marked. That's all you need to be looking for. If you're still having trouble, contact your local Family Support Center. Often they have classes for new spouses and how to read an LES is one of the topics covered.

Financial Counseling

Each Family Support Center and the nonprofit attached to your branch offers financial counseling and budget preparation help. You can find the local office for your branch's nonprofit at:

Army Emergency Relief (AER): www.aerhq.org

Air Force Aid Society (AFAS): www.afas.org

Coast Guard Mutual Assistance (CGMA): www.cgmahq.org

Navy Marine Corps Relief Society (NMCRS): www.nmcrs.org

Even if you don't want to create a budget with a financial advisor, they can give you the form and you can complete it in your own time. However, I do suggest you take advantage of their expertise, particularly if you've got a major change coming (such as a new baby or a child going to college).

The most important thing about creating a budget is being realistic. Look at your previous month's bills and bank statements to see just how much you spend on incidentals.

For example, if you and your spouse each get a $4 latte on the way to work every day, that's $40 a week, or $120 a month just on morning coffee! Once you find nonessential expenses like this, you can limit them and use the money more productively. Half the battle is realizing what you're spending your money on.

Debt Reduction

Once you've completed your budget, you'll know exactly what you're paying each month in debt. So now it's time to look at what you can do about it. Here is an example of a debt table. Yes, this is quite typical. Each of the interest rates were obtained from the companies websites in November 2007.

Debt Pay-Off Timeframe

Type of Debt	Lender/Store	Interest Rate	Balance	Monthly Payment	Time to Pay Off
Credit Card	Navy Federal C.U.	7.90%	$1,500	$35.00	4 yrs, 3 mos
Store Card	Home Depot	19%	$2,000	$50.00	5 yrs, 4 mos
Store Card	Sears	24.65%	$500	$20.00	3 yrs
Home Equity Loan	Navy Federal C.U.	6.75%	$7,670	$115.00	7 yrs
Student Loan	Chase/Stafford Loan	7.22%	$16,000	$219.00	8 yrs
Car Loan	USAA	5.44%	$10,500	$275.12	3 yrs, 6 mos
Car Loan	Navy Federal C.U.	4.25%	$6,000	$261.22	2 yrs

To calculate the amount of time to pay off your credit cards, go to www.ditech.com/calculators/creditcard.html. I've not personally used Ditech as a lender, but I do love their credit card payment calculator.

Look at the table. This person has a $500 balance on his Sears card. Because he is making minimum payments of $20 a month, it's going to take three years to pay off his balance. $20 × 36 months = $720. So he's paying an extra $220 in interest alone!

Using Ditech's calculator, you can see what increasing the monthly payment will do to the number of months needed to pay it off, or even specify how soon you want it paid off, and it will show you how much you need to pay per month to reach that goal.

Top's Tips

You should always have a buffer in savings that can be accessed immediately for emergency use. Three months' worth of expenses is the standard amount most financial experts suggest. That can be quite a challenge for junior military families, but it is worth working toward this goal.

So long as you have at least one month's worth of expenses in savings, and you're adding to it every month, it's worth looking at your debt and how you can pay it down. Accruing 5 percent interest in a savings account doesn't make sense if you've got a credit card that you're paying 25 percent interest on. Get rid of the lowest balances with the highest interest rates first.

Let's say that the person in the table worked out his budget and found an extra $100 a month that he can use to pay down bills. Let's look at what he can do with that.

For five months, he puts it toward his Sears card. Now, that card is completely paid off and he's got $120 to use (because he doesn't have the $20 a month going to the Sears card anymore).

Now he puts that $120 toward his Home Depot Card (the next-highest interest rate). Fourteen months later, his Home Depot card is paid off and he's now got $170 he can use to pay down other bills. In less than 18 months, he's cleared 2 cards and saved himself $940 in interest alone!

Now he can put that $170 toward his remaining credit card and pay that off in eight months. Now he's got $205 a month extra and no debt that has an interest rate over 8 percent. Eventually, he will have paid off all of his debt much earlier and he can start really building up his savings account (past the three months' emergency fund).

Making the Most of Your TSP

Your Thrift Savings Plan (TSP) is like a 401k retirement fund. Your spouse can allocate a percentage of his or her basic pay or special pays and bonuses to go directly to the TSP pretax. You can manage your TSP online and select your own portfolio to low risk, medium risk, or high risk, depending on how close you are to retirement. Just like with a 401k, you cannot withdraw from the TSP except under certain circumstances (financial hardship is one of them), so this is not a regular savings account.

I am not a financial expert, and certainly not a stocks expert, but this is something that I strongly suggest you look into. The maximum 2008 contributions are $15,500 for taxable pay and $46,000 for tax-free pay. No matter where you are in your career, saving for retirement (at age 60, not military retirement) is something you need to consider. You can learn more at www.tsp.gov.

The Least You Need to Know

◆ Pay is taxable, but allowances are nontaxable.

◆ When your spouse is deployed in a hazard duty zone, his pay becomes nontaxable.

◆ Have your spouse talk to his career counselor to see if he's eligible for a reenlistment bonus (SRB).

◆ Create a realistic budget that you can stick to.

◆ Creating a debt table and calculating when you will pay off each item can help you focus on your finances better.

◆ Start saving for retirement using a TSP fund.

Chapter 3

Benefits for Military Families

In This Chapter

- ◆ Saving money by shopping on base
- ◆ VA home loans, who is eligible, and how to apply
- ◆ How the military helps you get your education
- ◆ Additional health-care coverage
- ◆ Base housing and how privatization affects you
- ◆ Space-available airline travel

We covered the pay and allowances that your spouse receives in his paycheck in Chapter 2, but that is really just the tip of the iceberg. In this chapter, we cover other financial benefits of being part of a military family. Some of these you might already know, but by the end of this chapter I hope you have a better understanding of how these benefits work.

The Shopaholic's Dream

Military families enjoy tax-free shopping on-base. Shopping discounts are a huge financial benefit for military families. You can save thousands on your shopping bills. My local sales tax rate is 8.3 percent, so removing that is like shopping during a sale every day. Plus the prices are usually a lot lower than in other stores. And they will price-match if you do find an item cheaper elsewhere.

Even if you're overseas, you will have a Commissary (and usually a small Exchange), but you can shop online, too.

Shopping at the Exchange

The Exchange is a department store. You'll find electronics, adults' and kids' clothing, sporting goods, toys, household goods, furniture, DVDs, computers, garden items, etc. The name of the Exchange (and who manages it) depends on which branch of the military runs the base you are stationed at (it's not always the branch your spouse is in). Here are the names you may see:

◆ Army: PX (Post Exchange)

◆ Air Force: BX (Base Exchange)

◆ Navy: NEX (Navy Exchange)

◆ Marine Corps: MCX (Marine Corps Exchange)

◆ Coast Guard: CGEX (Coast Guard Exchange)

The Army and Air Force exchanges are run by AAFES (Army and Air Force Exchange Service). The other Exchanges are run by companies with the same name as the store.

The Exchange is a great place to buy all kinds of items. The selection might not be as big as you'll find in the mall, but the prices are typically 20 percent lower than the competition. Plus you pay no tax, and they have pretty good sales, too.

You can also shop the Exchange online. The shipping cost (except for oversize items) is included in the price. There is a much bigger selection online. The online shopping Exchanges have merged, so now there is just one site called the All Services Exchange Online Store at https://thor.milexch.com.

The Commissary

The Commissary is run by DeCA (Defense Commissary Agency). This is the grocery store for military families. The cost is far lower than any other grocery store, but (depending on the size) the selection may be limited. Still, it's worth the savings! According to DeCA, military families save an average of over 30 percent, which they say translates to about $3,000 a year for a typical family of four. Not bad, really.

You don't pay sales tax at the Commissary, but you do pay a 5 percent surcharge fee. The Commissary is government subsidized, and Congress mandated that this fee be charged to help pay for Commissary building construction, repairs, etc.

The Commissary and Exchange do not price-match with each other. So compare both prices (remember the Exchange doesn't have a surcharge). Their locations are usually very close anyway (often sharing a parking lot) so it's not a big deal to go to both during one shopping trip.

Both the Commissary and Exchange take order requests. So if an item is in their system they can usually order it for you.

VA Home Loans

The Department of Veterans Affairs (VA) provides programs and assistance to military veterans. A VA loan is guaranteed by the government, which enables you to get a lower interest rate with less money down. The VA inspects and appraises the property and your purchase price cannot be higher than this appraisal.

All active-duty and former active-duty (retired or not) are eligible for a VA loan. Certain reserve and

 Ask the Chief _____

A VA loan is not actually a loan through the VA. It is from a regular lender, but the loan is guaranteed by the government. So if you don't pay, the mortgage holder is still guaranteed the funds.

National Guard personnel are also eligible for VA loans. You can read more about this at www.homeloans.va.gov/faqelig.htm.

How to Apply

You will need a Certificate of Eligibility. This can be requested by submitting VA form 26-1880 (available at www.vba.va.gov/pubs/forms/vba-26-1880-ARE.pdf) and mailing it along with a Statement of Service from your spouse's unit or command to prove his eligibility.

It shouldn't take long to get it back, but you'd be wise to get the certificate in hand before you start home shopping.

If your lender has access to the ACE system (Automatic Certificate of Eligibility), which most do, they can print it out for you while you wait.

How Many Times Can You Use It?

Your VA Certificate of Eligibility can only be used on one home at a time. So if you buy a home using a VA loan, and put renters in when you move to another station, you cannot then buy another home at your new duty station with a VA loan. If you sold the old house, you can apply to have your VA eligibility reinstated, and then use it again for the next home loan. You must close on the first home to release your VA eligibility before closing on your new home.

Fire in the Hole!

To reinstate the VA loan eligibility, you must have paid off the loan when you sold the house. If the buyer assumes your loan, rather than getting a new one, you will not be able to use your VA loan eligibility until that loan is completely paid off. However, if the person assuming your loan also has a VA Certificate of Eligibility and is willing to substitute his into the assumed loan then yours is free for you to use again.

For information about the fees the lender can charge borrowers using a VA loan, go to www.valoans.com/va_facts_closing.cfm.

Free Legal Assistance

Most bases have a legal office. The attorneys cannot represent you in court, but they can advise you on many civil issues. They can provide power of attorneys, wills and trusts, notary services, read over lease and purchase agreements, help with immigration, and help in legal separations and divorce.

Legal services are free, and both the military member and spouse can request their assistance. If there is a legal issue between two eligible people (husband and wife, two military members, etc.), they cannot advise both of you. The first person to MEET with an attorney at the office establishes an attorney-client relationship. If you approach legal and are told "you've been conflicted out" that means they are already advising someone involved in that legal situation. They can give you a referral to another military legal office, but this could take awhile.

Some bases offer walk-in services, but most require you to make an appointment. It can take a couple of weeks to get an appointment for nonurgent assistance (such as creating a will), so make sure you get booked in well before you need it.

Family Education Programs

Each service branch has a form of Servicemembers Opportunity College (SOC). These are colleges that guarantee military members and their families can continue their Associate's or Bachelor's degree without losing credits when they change duty stations. This is particularly useful for part-time students who have little chance of completing a degree in one tour of duty.

These colleges usually have an office on-base, and many degree programs can be completed online.

The name of the program varies by branch, but the services are very similar. For more information, go to your branch's website.

Servicemember Opportunity College Information for Each Branch

Branch	Name	Website
Air Force	SOC	www.soc.aascu.org
Army	SOCAD	www.soc.aascu.org/socad
Navy	SOCNAV	www.soc.aascu.org/socnav
Marine Corps	SOCMAR	www.soc.aascu.org/socmar
Coast Guard	SOCCOAST	www.soc.aascu.org/soccoast
National Guard	SOCGuard	www.soc.aascu.org/socguard

Scholarship Programs

The Vice Admiral E. P. Travers Scholarship and Loan Program awards scholarships to spouses and children of active-duty members, and children of retired, or activated reserve (over 90 days) Sailors and Marines. The applicant must be a full-time student enrolled in an undergraduate degree program. Scholarships from $500 to $2,500 per academic year are awarded on a needs basis.

Interest-free loans up to $3,000 per year are also available. For more information, go to www.nmcrs.org/travers.

The Air Force Aid Society (www.afas.org) provides $2,000 grants through the General Henry H. Arnold Education Grant Program to spouses and children of active-duty, retired, and reservist Air Force. The grants are awarded on a needs basis.

Army Emergency Relief (www.aerhq.org) offers Stateside Spouse Education Assistance Program (SSEAP) scholarships to full-time student spouses of active-duty and retired Army personnel living in the United States.

Coast Guard Mutual Assistance (CGMA) offers a Supplemental Education Grant (SEG) to active-duty, retired, selected reserve Coast Guard, and their family members (restrictions apply). The applicant must be enrolled in an undergraduate degree program, be working toward their GED, or an approved vocational program.

The maximum $160 grant is for nontuition expenses—textbooks, registration, lab fees, study guides, etc. For more information go to www.cgmahq.org/Assistance/categories/attachments/seg.pdf.

If you get a Federal Stafford or PLUS student loan, CGMA will reimburse the 3 percent origination fee that you paid. The same eligibility requirements apply as for the SEG.

The VOTECH Student Loan Program will loan qualifying students of approved programs up to $1,500. Active-duty, spouses, and children of Coast Guard members are eligible, but there must be a demonstrated financial need for the assistance.

To find out more about all of the CGMA education programs go to www.cgmahq.org, clicking on the Assistance tab, and then Education.

CLEP Tests

CLEP (College Level Examination Program) tests are widely accepted in lieu of college course credits for lower-level required courses (English, Math, etc.). They are free for active-duty, and cost $65 for spouses. That's a lot less than you would pay for a college course, even at a community college. Your on-base college learning center may administer CLEP tests. If not, most community colleges offer them.

Montgomery GI Bill

The Montgomery GI Bill is very convoluted and is something your spouse must have signed up for during basic training/boot camp. All branches now offer 100 percent Tuition Assistance (TA) while they are on active-duty, so most military members wait until after they leave the military to use their GI Bill allowances.

You can read about it at www.gibill.va.gov. I'm not going to cover all the details here, because it generally doesn't apply to spouses.

Having said that, the Army is currently testing a retention program that enables a qualifying enlisted soldier to transfer up to 50 percent of his GI Bill entitlement to his spouse.

There are a lot of restrictions to this program and many people do not qualify. The program is designed as an incentive for soldiers in critically manned jobs to reenlist. The reenlistment bonus (SRB) is lower, but it is an incentive worthwhile to many soldiers. None of the other branches have a program like this yet.

There are many other tuition assistance programs for spouses living overseas, which we cover in Chapter 10.

Subsidized Childcare

Many bases have a DOD-run Child Development Center that takes children from six weeks to pre-K. The price you pay is based on your total household income. The fee you pay is recalculated once a year.

Most bases also have in-home childcare programs (called Family Child Care or Child Development Homes), and also after-school programs for school-aged children. We'll discuss this in more detail in Chapter 6.

Vision Services

If you have TRICARE Prime and you wear glasses, you are eligible for one free eye test per year. You can see any optician who accepts TRICARE. There's no claim to file and no co-pay. Just make sure you have your military ID card with you.

But, your actual glasses are not free. Many Exchanges have an optical shop where you can get glasses or contact lenses, but the selection is often limited to the more expensive brands.

Contact lens prescriptions are not covered by TRICARE. However, most opticians will give you one if you express interest in contact lenses because they want you to buy them from their store.

Dental Services

The TRICARE Dental Program (TDP) is managed by United Concordia. This is not an automatic benefit—your spouse must set up an allotment to pay for it. TDP is open to reservists, National Guard, and active-duty families, but the premiums vary.

The monthly premium depends on the number of people in your family that are covered by the policy. If your spouse is active-duty, he is already covered for dental on-base. So, to cover you (or any *one* family member) the fee is $11.58 per month. If you need coverage for more than one person, the family policy is $28.95 per month, whether you have two dependents or five.

If your spouse is National Guard or Selected Reserve, the premiums are ...

TRICARE Dental Premium Rates for National Guard and Reservists

Who is Covered	National Guard/ Selected Reserve	Individual Ready Reserve
Sponsor only	$11.58	$28.95
One family member (not incl. sponsor)	$28.95	$28.95
Sponsor and one family member	$40.53	$57.90
All family members (not incl. sponsor)	$72.37	$72.37
Sponsor and all family members	$83.95	$101.32

Note: All of the premiums in this section are for the enrollment period February 21, 2008 through January 31, 2009.

How to Determine Your Co-Pays

Diagnostic, preventative, and emergency dental services have no co-pay. All other covered services have co-pays ranging from 20 to 50 percent. Co-pays for endodontic, periodontic, and oral surgery are 10 percent less for E4 and below.

To view the full co-pays list or to check for updated premium costs, go to www.tricaredentalprogram.com. Click on Enrollees, and then select Cost Shares/Premiums on the left sidebar, and then select whichever you are looking for.

Finding a Dental Provider

You can find a TRICARE-network dentist online at www.
tricaredentalprogram.com. Click Find a Dentist to search by specialty,
or by provider name if you want to check if a recommended dentist is in
the TRICARE Dental network.

Base Housing

Base housing is often a housing development off-base. It is currently
being privatized, which means some changes are coming.

Ask the Chief

There are different names
for this program. The Navy
calls it PPV (Public/Private
Venture), Army calls it RCI
(Residential Community
Initiative), and Air Force calls
it HP (Housing Privatization).
They all mean the same
thing.

Until now, families who lived in
base housing forfeited their Basic
Allowance for Housing (BAH) to the
government in exchange for living in
base housing. Until the full privatization is complete, this will be very
similar, except that you will receive
the BAH payment, but it will never
actually get to your bank account
because an automatic allotment will
send the payment straight to the new
management company.

Utility Bills

Another change is the introduction of paying utilities. Currently, the
full cost is covered and residents don't even see how much they are
using. The management company will establish a baseline for utility
cost in that area (similar to how they establish BAH rates); 110 percent
of that amount will be deducted from the rent allotment.

So if your BAH is $1000 and the 110 percent utility allowance is $200,
then your rent allotment to the management company will be $800.
You keep the remaining $200 to pay your utility bills.

The idea is that those in base housing will become aware of the financial benefit they are receiving by living in base housing. By privatizing
housing, the DoD also expects the quality of housing and maintenance
to improve.

What Base Housing Privatization Means to You

Right now, privatization means a change in whom you contact for maintenance issues and (hopefully) much better customer service.

Not all bases have been privatized yet. So you might move into housing under the old system, and it change while you're there.

No locations have started the utilities allowance as of this writing. Until that happens, your spouse's LES will show the BAH payment, and then all of it will be sent to the management via allotment (because they are currently paying the utility bills). Once you start receiving a utility allowance, any usage over that amount is paid out of your pocket.

Military Flights

You'll hear various names for this: Space-A, NALO, MAC flights, etc., but they are all essentially the same thing.

You can fly space-available on many flights from military bases. There are restrictions, including that your sponsor must be with you if you're flying within the United States.

If you are flying overseas, it is possible to use military flights without your sponsor, but only if the flight you are on goes directly overseas. So you can't fly from the west coast to the east coast, change planes, and then fly to Europe.

However, if the same plane is just refueling on the east coast and you will not change planes, that's okay.

The fee is very minimal and, depending on the circumstances, it may actually be free. The most I've seen is $50. Considering the cost of flying these days, that is very reasonable.

The Air Force has a great publication all about Space-A travel. The direct link is: www.amc.af.mil/shared/media/document/AFD-060328-001.doc.

You will never get a schedule of flights online for OPSEC reasons. It's just not going to happen because of operational security (OPSEC) concerns after 9/11. The best way to find out about flights is to visit your local terminal. Usually a schedule is available 5-14 days in advance.

At www.spacea.net/locations you will find a directory with phone numbers and the bases they are attached to. There's a lot of other information on www.spacea.net that you will probably find of interest.

Never rely on Space-A travel. You can never guarantee you will be able to get on a flight, and if your spouse is due back at work, you may have to buy him a commercial ticket to get him back on time (and you, too, as you can't fly Space-A within the United States without him). This is very expensive. So just allow a good amount of time after the end of your trip for him to get home.

The Least You Need to Know

◆ Shopping at the Exchange saves an average of 20 percent off retail prices, plus there is no sales tax.

◆ Shopping at the Commissary saves an average of 30 percent on grocery bills, but there is a 5 percent surcharge.

◆ You can only use your spouse's VA loan eligibility one active mortgage at a time.

◆ Subsidized childcare is available, but the waiting list is based on priority factors.

◆ TRICARE dental is available for active-duty, reserve, and National Guard personnel, but the monthly premiums vary.

◆ Space-available military flights are great, but you shouldn't rely on them for time-critical travel.

Chapter 4

Military Family Support Services

In This Chapter

- ◆ How to find your local Family Support Center
- ◆ Programs and services offered by your Family Service Center
- ◆ How to get free childcare before your PCS move
- ◆ Programs and assistance provided by your branch's charity organization
- ◆ Emergency financial aid programs

The Family Support Center is a lifeline for spouses, yet many people have no idea about the variety of programs and services available to them through this on-base resource.

This chapter gives you an overview of the services offered by both your Family Support Center and the nonprofit organization attached to your branch of service.

Family Support Centers

Gone are the days of "if the military wanted you to have a wife, they'd have issued you one." Now, although families are not the number one priority of the military, we are no longer neglected.

Almost all bases have a Family Support Center of some kind. Some are bigger than others, but they all offer a wide variety of programs for military families.

Different Names for Different Branches

Although I use the generic name "Family Support Center," your center's actual name will depend on your branch of service.

Army: Army Community Service Center

Navy: Fleet and Family Support Center

Air Force: Airman and Family Readiness Center

Coast Guard: Work-Life Center

Marine Corps: Marine Corps Community Services

National Guard: Family Assistance Center

You can find your local Family Support Center at www.militaryinstallations.dod.mil by selecting Family Center from the Program or Service menu, and then selecting your branch of service and/or specific location. Other branch Family Support Centers can and will help you, so don't worry if your unit or command is only a small one on another branch's base.

For the National Guard, the programs are the same, but finding the office locations is a little different.

1. Go to www.guardfamily.org/Public/Application/ResourceFinderSearch.aspx

2. Select a state from the map, or use the menu list.

3. If you know there is a location in your city, you can select it from the list. Alternatively, skip this box and move on to the next one.

4. In the Category menu, select Family Assistance Center.

5. Click Submit.

If you selected the specific city, the Family Support Center in that location will display. If you selected just the state, you'll get a list of all of the locations in that state.

Most of the programs are very similar across branches because they are organized by the Department of Defense and then operated by each Family Support Center.

You may find your center has additional programs, but most offer all of the ones I will be discussing (although the name may be slightly different).

Family Employment Readiness Program (FERP)

This is an important program for relocated spouses. If you wish to work in the local community, it can be quite a challenge to find an appropriate job. The FERP will assist you with your resumé, cover letters, and interview technique, as well as with offering career counseling services.

They have listings of local jobs, and have computers available for online job searches and for creating resumés and cover letters. It is usually run by the same team that manages the Transition Assistance Program (which helps active-duty members transition to civilian work life when they leave the military).

One of the things I like about FERP is they also have information about on-base jobs and even federal jobs. It's certainly worth a look if you're trying to find a job. You can find more about this program at the MilitaryHOMEFRONT website, www.militaryhomefront.dod. mil. Click Troops and Families (in the top navigation bar) and then Employment (in the left sidebar).

Relocation Assistance Program (RAP)

Many, but not all, Family Support Centers offer a relocation program to help you when you're transferring from one base to another. These are the people who provide your welcome packet with information about the new base and surrounding area. They often have a selection of household essential items that you can borrow until your household goods shipment arrives (it's usually called a Lending Locker).

Top's Tips

If you find a website link that doesn't exist anymore (for any family-related program), the likelihood is that you'll now find the information on www.militaryhomefront.dod.mil or www.militaryonesource.com.

You may see information about SITES online, or in pamphlets given to you by your command. This used to be the online source for information about relocation. In 2006, the DoD ended the SITES program and now provides this information through www.militaryonesource.com and www.militaryhomefront.dod.mil.

Personal Financial Management (PFM)

You can talk to a financial counselor individually, or attend a group class. They can help you create a budget, manage your debt, work out a plan for a large expense, etc.

Counseling (Marriage, Personal, Children, etc.)

Life in the military is stressful for both the active-duty member and his family. Sometimes you need to speak to someone confidentially. The Family Support Center has a professional counseling team who specializes in various different areas, from marriage counseling, to bereavement, personal issues, or helping a troubled child. All services are free and confidential.

Free courses are also available for a variety of life skills to make military life easier. For example, you can take courses for helping build communication between you and your spouse.

New Parent Support Program (NPS)

I cannot praise the New Parent Support Program highly enough. They are a fantastic resource for all new parents, in fact, they work with parents with children from birth to three years.

They provide developmental resources as well as working through a curriculum that helps you discover new ways to stimulate your child's learning. They conduct regular developmental questionnaires, which helps you see where your child is in relation to "typical" children of that age.

You will receive regular informal home visits, the frequency will depend on the caseload, and your level of need. The providers are very friendly and you can ask them questions that maybe you wouldn't want to bother your pediatrician with.

Family Advocacy Programs (FAS)

Family Advocacy offers tools to help prevent, identify, and deal with the aftermath of spousal or child abuse.

They offer many programs, and in fact, the New Parent Support Program comes under Family Advocacy because it helps you learn how to deal with the challenges of being a parent, rather than letting it get to a point where you can't cope anymore.

There are prevention programs, stress-management programs, as well as educational programs targeted at the commands regarding the reporting of suspected abuse. There are also victim-support services and emergency-placement services for children at risk.

Exceptional Family Member Program (EFM)

An Exceptional Family Member is any dependent with a special need. It could be physical, developmental, educational, or medical. Once a special need is identified, enrollment in the EFM program is mandatory.

This information is used to ensure that when you PCS, your new location can accommodate your family member appropriately.

There is a liaison person from the EFM program at each Family Service Center, but often the program is actually managed at your base hospital or other military treatment facility.

Nonprofit Relief Societies

Each branch of the military has its own charity. They offer financial support and education scholarships, as well as other support services. Each charity's services are slightly different. They all focus on essential short-term and emergency assistance.

Army Emergency Relief (AER)

Army Emergency Relief (AER) is primarily focused on emergency and educational financial aid. They offer emergency money for household expenses (rent, utilities, food), medical/dental expenses, emergency travel or vehicle repair, funeral expenses, and personal needs if your spouse's pay is delayed or stolen.

The financial aid may be in the form of an interest-free loan, or a grant, or a combination of the two.

If you are in need of assistance from AER, you can find your local office at www.aerhq.org/section_locations.asp. You will need a Power of Attorney if your spouse is deployed and unable to attend the appointment, because, if you receive a loan, you will need to set up a repayment allotment from his pay.

Air Force Aid Society (AFAS)

The Air Force Aid Society (AFAS) offer interest-free loans and grants just like AER, and for pretty much all the same situations. They also offer many community programs. These include the following:

Respite Care—A grant to families caring for a chronically ill relative to pay for alternative care for a few hours each week, to give your family a break.

Give Parents a Break—AFAS pays for the Child Development Center to open at a nonregular time (often an evening or weekend morning) once a month for childcare for families undergoing particular stress (deployments, sick relative, etc.). This gives the eligible parents a few hours of time off without the kids, to get things done or just have a break from the additional stresses of being a parent.

Bundles for Babies—AFAS provides a bag filled with new Gerber brand layette items to new parents. The bundle includes blankets, onesies, cloth diapers, booties, etc. These are distributed through the Family Support Center.

Car Care Because We Care—This program offers grants for vehicle preventative maintenance when the active-duty member is deployed for over 30 days or stationed in a remote location overseas on a 1-year unaccompanied tour. It pays for oil, lube, and filter services, and (in some Northern states) winterizing for the primary family vehicle.

Child Care for PCS—Parents can receive a certificate for 20 hours of childcare at a Family Child Care (FCC) home or other authorized Air Force childcare facility to use within the last 60 days before a PCS move. You can also receive a 20-hour certificate at your new base to use while you're moving in and unpacking. Unused hours from the departing base cannot be used at the new base, so you have to get the second certificate. If there is a shortage of childcare spaces, priority will be given to junior enlisted members.

Phone Home—AFAS provides $20 phone cards to deploying active-duty (and activated Air National Guard and reserve) Air Force members so they can call home. These cards are distributed through the Family Support Center.

Heart Link—This is a spouse orientation program. The idea is to help spouses understand and acclimatize to the military way of life. Funding for this program is provided, in part, by AFAS, although they do not provide the program itself.

Some of these programs require referrals from the command, Family Advocacy, or the Exception Family Member Program officer, but you can find out by calling your local AFAS location.

For more information about AFAS community programs go to www. afas.org and click on Community Programs. To find your local AFAS office, go to www.afas.org/location/location.cfm.

Coast Guard Mutual Assistance (CGMA)

Coast Guard Mutual Assistance provides various financial services including emergency financial aid (pretty much the same as AER) and a few other programs.

Financial Counseling and Debt Management—Provides individual financial planning help, but can also help a person get into a program such as the Consumer Credit Counseling Service (CCCS), which has a minimum financial commitment.

Housing Assistance—Helps a qualifying individual with one-time expenses related to buying a house, renting a property, or setting up utility services.

Layette Program—This provides layette items (onesies, blankets, etc.) to E3-and-below active-duty Coast Guard members.

Survivor Benefit Assistance—Provides assistance for widows who have lost their spouse during active-duty (or activated reserve). It helps the spouse understand the benefits available to her and how to proceed with the administration process through the Department of Veterans Affairs, Social Security Administration, and Survivor Benefit Plan.

You can find out more about the CGMA's programs at www.cgmahq. org. Click Assistance, then Categories, and then select the program that interests you.

To find your closest CGMA location, go to www.cgmahq.org and click Contacting Us, then Representatives, and then select CGMA Locations and Representatives.

Navy Marine Corps Relief Society (NMCRS)

The Navy Marine Corps Relief Society (NMCRS) provides services to both Sailors and Marines. They offer emergency financial aid, just like the other branch's charities. In January 2008 they launched a new program called the Quick Assist Loan (QAL). This enables the active-duty member (not spouses) to receive an interest-free loan for up to $300 within 15 minutes. This was developed as an alternative to high-interest payday loans.

There are a number of other services and programs provided by the NMCRS:

Budget for Baby—New or soon-to-be parents can attend the group class, or work one on one. They will help you create a budget that includes the additional expenses associated with having a child. You will receive a "Baby's First Seabag," which includes various layette items.

Survivor Benefit Information—The NMCRS provides the same services as the CGMA.

Food Lockers—Some locations have volunteer-run food lockers that provide nutritional food to families who need that type of assistance. Infant formula and diapers may be available. If your location doesn't have a Food Locker, they can issue you a check payable to the Commissary to pay for the items you need.

Thrift Shop—The NMCRS volunteers operate a thrift store on many bases. This is a great place to get spare uniforms for your spouse very cheaply. They also have children's items as well as usual thrift-store household stuff. You can see which bases have NMCRS thrift stores at www.nmcrs.org/thriftshop.

Visiting Nurse—The Visiting Nurse program is designed to provide education about health issues and health-related resources for children. They provide home visits to families who live within a 25-mile radius of the base.

Go to www.nmcrs.org to find out more about these programs or to locate an office.

If you are stationed on a base that is not run by the branch of service your spouse is attached to, you can still receive financial aid. For example, if you're Air Force living on a Navy base, the NMCRS will provide the funds, but it will be transferred to the AFAS so you would repay the AFAS.

Online Support Services

There are two sites the military uses to provide information to military families. They are www.militaryonesource.com and www. militaryhomefront.dod.mil. These two sites cover pretty much everything relating to military life. When you register with Military One Source you identify your branch of service. From then on, it only shows you information relevant to your branch.

Military OneSource also has a toll-free number to assist you, and it is manned 24 hours a day, 365 days a year. The number is 1-800-342-9647.

Military Homefront covers quality-of-life topics. Click on Troops and Families to see the programs most tailored to the families.

Military.com is not run by the military, but is another useful source. I've found that most of the information is current, but because it's not an official DoD site, I find it useful to look at a topic on there, and then verify it with another source, just in case something has changed.

Milspouse.org is a great source for relocation, education, and employment information. It's very easy to look up resources in these three areas at your current installation, or one you're PCSing to. They have both CONUS and OCONUS information.

There are various message forums for military families. These include www.militarysos.com and www.cinchouse.com. Just remember anyone can read what you post, so don't put anything that could affect OPSEC. PLEASE no tickers counting the days until your spouse returns from deployment (this goes for MySpace, too).

As you can see, there are many resources available to spouses. I strongly recommend you always get the final word about a program or benefit from the organization that actually provides it. So, this way, you know you're getting the most current and accurate information.

The Least You Need to Know

- ◆ Your Family Support Center offers many programs, including family advocacy, counseling, new parent support, financial planning, job search assistance, etc.

- ◆ The branch-specific charities all offer financial aid in the form of grants and interest-free loans, but many also offer other services and programs.

- ◆ If you don't have your branch's charity on your base, you can get help from a charity attached to another branch.

- ◆ Many website resources have been consolidated into www. militaryonesource.com and www.militaryhomefront.dod.mil.

Chapter 5

You and Me Plus Baby Makes Three

In This Chapter

- ◆ Military care during and after pregnancy
- ◆ How to plan for the financial impact of children
- ◆ Free classes held at your local military hospital
- ◆ Registering a U.S. birth overseas
- ◆ What WIC covers and who is eligible
- ◆ How to get a bigger unit in base housing

Having a child will have a huge impact on your family dynamic as well as your budget. But there is good news: unlike in the civilian world where prenatal care is expensive, if you have TRICARE Prime, everything is covered. Even if you're TRICARE Standard, the co-pays are minimal.

What to Expect During Prenatal Care at a Military Hospital

"Military health care is substandard to civilian," "You don't get the proper care for your child at a military hospital," "Civilian hospitals are much better for Labor and Delivery." Those are just three of the statements I hear frequently, usually from people who have never actually experienced the care at both a military and civilian hospital, so can't really make an accurate comparison.

I received prenatal care at both, and chose to deliver my child at the military hospital. Every clinic is different, so you will need to use your own judgment, but it's very easy to get that impression from the first few visits.

I delivered my daughter at Naval Hospital Pensacola in 2006. I can say without a doubt that the OB-GYN and Pediatrics clinics there were the best departments I visited. I was thoroughly happy with every part of my prenatal and postpartum care, and with how all of the pediatricians took care of my daughter.

Because this is the only hospital where I've delivered a child, I can't say if civilian would have been better or worse for Labor and Delivery, but I did visit one of the other local hospitals where a civilian friend delivered her daughter (a month after my daughter was born) and the room was much smaller, the services were not as good, and it was very expensive for her, even though she didn't have a complicated delivery.

Family Practice vs. OB Clinic

You can choose whether to have your prenatal care through your Family Practice doctor or through the Obstetrics clinic. If you have a high-risk pregnancy, they will usually refer you to Obstetrics (OB) automatically, but anyone can request to be seen by an OB.

Some OB clinics have midwives as well as obstetricians. Midwives are usually female and tend to be less clinical or hurried, with a more personable and relaxed bedside manner. It's typically easier to get an appointment with a midwife than an OB.

It's entirely up to you which you choose. If you're interested in using a midwife, ask the nurse at your first appointment if your clinic has one and who it is.

Free Classes at Your Hospital

Every hospital offers many free classes that our civilian counterparts must pay for. Even if you decide to have your main care off-base, you can still take part in the on-base classes.

Some typical classes include the following:

◆ Childbirth preparation

◆ Red Cross infant first aid

◆ Breastfeeding

◆ Infant care

◆ Sibling care (for kids ages three to nine, to prepare for a new baby in the household)

◆ New dad's preparation

Your OB clinic will have the class schedule. You'll usually have to register ahead. Each class typically has a "goodie bag" with tons of samples, which lets you try different brands without buying a full pack of any particular product.

Ultrasounds

You will get one ultrasound around 20 weeks. This will be usually done on-base. If you're a higher risk, they may decide you need a level 2 or level 3 ultrasound, in which case you'll usually be seen by a specialist off-base.

You may receive more than one ultrasound. If you're seen in the OB clinic, they usually have a small ultrasound machine. In this case you might get an ultrasound before 20 weeks.

Off-Base Referrals

If your OB has a concern outside his specialty, or your hospital doesn't have a piece of testing equipment he needs, you will be referred off-base to a specialist. In this situation, you will pay a $12 co-pay at the time of the visit. You will continue to be seen for most appointments by your regular OB.

What to Expect During the Delivery

Unless you have a scheduled caesarian section, you cannot guarantee who will actually deliver your child. In a military hospital, it is whoever is on duty at Labor and Delivery when you are ready to push.

Your Room

If you attend childbirth classes, you'll get a tour of Labor and Delivery, so you will see the room before you're in labor. Typically it will have your bed, a rocking chair/glider, a chair that converts into a bed, a TV, CD player, and a mini-fridge. You'll also have an ensuite bathroom. Some have bathtubs, and others have showers with seats.

You may get to stay in the same room for your entire stay (labor, delivery, and postdelivery care), but if Labor and Delivery is busy you may be asked to move rooms during recovery. This is because they try to keep laboring women in adjacent rooms. This makes it much easier for the nurses and OBs to give the necessary care to each woman in labor without wasting time rushing down corridors to get to the next room.

Seating is limited so if you expect lots of visitors, bring folding chairs with you. This way you won't have people perching on the end of your bed.

Pain Medication

If you plan to have an epidural, make sure you read the form they give you to sign and ensure that your name is spelled as it is registered in DEERS.

It takes about an hour after the blood reaches the lab to get it processed and the results entered into the computer. If your name on the vials of blood doesn't match what is in the computer, the lab has to throw out the blood work (which they will have already tested) and start again. This could mean a delay of an hour or two for you getting your pain medication. It's much better to check the spelling on the form.

I made this mistake (the form said "Lisa," not "Lissa"). Let's just say, if you want timely pain meds, then check the form!

Who Will Deliver Your Child?

Midwives can do most deliveries. They can do a vacuum delivery, but not forceps. They can also cut an episiotomy, but not repair it. So if you need any of these, there will be an obstetrician on hand who will take care of the parts midwives are not allowed to do. C-sections are always performed by an obstetrician. I was lucky that my OB was on duty when I went into labor, and my midwife was able to be there for the actual delivery too, but it doesn't always work out that way.

How Long Will You Stay?

Different states have different regulations for how long you (or the baby) must stay. They may decide to keep you longer if you have complications, but most of the time they'll let you go after the minimum time.

While you're in the hospital, take advantage of the experts around you. There is a lactation consultant (usually the same person who gave the breastfeeding class) who will help you if you're having trouble. The nurses will often monitor your baby for a few hours so you can get some sleep each night.

The cart will be full of diapers, wipes, etc. Use them! You're going to go through tons of diapers and wipes at your own expense, so why not use the ones provided.

Postpartum Care

Your child will be seen three days after birth and then in frequent intervals after that. You will have checkups with your OB, too. Being a new parent is challenging, so if you need help, ask. This is not the time to be a tough-as-nails military wife.

Pediatrics or Family Practice

If you decided to stick with a family practice doctor throughout your prenatal care, your doctor should be able to see your child as well. If not, your child will be assigned to Pediatrics.

You will need to visit your TRICARE office to add your child onto the policy. Do this ASAP because you need your child's checkups to be covered by TRICARE. At this time you can select Pediatrics, a specific pediatrician, or your family practice doctor. If you were seen in Family Practice, but want your child to be seen in the Pediatric clinic, that's completely fine.

What If My Spouse Is Having the Baby?

If the active-duty member is female, then you can expect the same level of care for her. She will not return to work until six weeks after your child is born. She will also be nondeployable for four months. She will be seen in the OB clinic, because active-duty do not see family practice doctors.

New Parent Support Program

I talked about the New Parent Support Program in Chapter 4. This is one of the best programs out there. It is not branch-specific so you should have it at your base.

They are incredibly helpful for nonmedical issues. Most of the case-workers are parents, too, so they've experienced most of what you're going through. They'll help you figure out how to handle all the changes in your life, how to take care of a child, and answer the million questions you will have.

They also provide age-appropriate developmental resources. They can refer you to other services if they think it's needed, too.

What If Your Spouse Is Deployed?

This is a very tough situation. Unfortunately the delivery of a child is not considered an emergency, and your spouse will not be pulled back from a deployment because of it.

Just remember, there are thousands of other military spouses who are in the same position as you. In this regard I think it's better to be at a military hospital. They are used to seeing pregnant women with a parent or friend instead of their husband.

It's definitely worth asking a close friend or family member to stay with you for awhile. It will really help after your baby is born. Take lots of photos and video clips for Dad to see when he does get home. He may even be able to coach you through your labor via phone, depending on where you are and where he is.

If you do have complications during delivery, then an American Red Cross message can be sent to your spouse, and there is a much higher chance that he will be brought home early. But they would need to be serious complications.

If you don't have a family member or friend who can help you during the delivery, you may be eligible to get support from a doula through Operation Special Delivery. Doula's are trained to assist women during Labor and Delivery. They are not medical staff; they are strictly support-orientated.

Usually a doula is quite expensive, but if your spouse is deployed in support of the War on Terrorism, you may be eligible to have a doula free of charge. You can find out more about this program at www. operationspecialdelivery.com.

What If You Are Stationed Overseas?

Your care will be from whichever treatment facility you usually use. It may be a military hospital or a local one. If you're concerned about local customs concerning childbirth, talk with your primary care provider. Most medical facilities near a U.S. military base have experience with American pregnant women and the customs we are used to. If there is something specific you do or don't want, make sure to tell your provider. It's much better to discuss it before you are in labor!

Registering the Birth of a U.S. Citizen

If either you or your spouse is a U.S. citizen, your child will automatically be a U.S. citizen at birth, no matter where in the world you are stationed.

You will still need to register your child's birth with your local U.S. Consulate. For specific instructions, go to www.travel.state.gov/law/info/overseas/overseas_703.html.

To find your local consulate, go to http://usembassy.state.gov. Once you get to the correct country page, the specific requirements for registering the birth of a U.S. citizen from that location will usually be found under Passport Services.

What Does Dual Citizenship Mean for Your Child?

The United States does not acknowledge dual citizenship. However, that doesn't mean that other countries don't. For example, my daughter is a dual citizen by birth. I am a British citizen. My husband is a U.S. citizen.

If the country you are in gives citizenship to all children born in that country, you may get a passport for your child from that country. However, you should still register her as a U.S. citizen and get her a U.S. passport. As far as the United States is concerned, the child is a U.S. citizen only. You may only travel to and from the United States using her U.S. passport. Not doing so could cause complications at immigration.

How Will Your Budget Change?

Your budget will change, there's no doubt about that. Diapers, wipes, clothes, food, formula, bottles, toys, nursery furniture, etc. It all adds up, and they only get more expensive. This is just the reality of parenting, but it's not difficult to budget for. You just need to prioritize your expenses.

You will likely find yourself not buying those cute shoes for yourself, but looking at baby sneakers, or a cute little outfit for your baby. This is a normal instinct—you want to provide for your child. You do need to be careful about how much you spend, though. It's tempting to buy lots of things, but realistically, your child will grow out of clothes within a few months, so is it really worth spending $30–$40 on an outfit?

I found buying used items was a huge money saver. Your child doesn't know the difference, and you can get some wonderful things at very low prices. I use craigslist.org, eBay.com, as well as the on-base charity shop and local consignment stores.

You should always check for recalls on any item you are considering purchasing used. You should also thoroughly inspect it for loose or broken parts, or other safety hazards.

 Fire in the Hole!

There are a few things you shouldn't buy used. They include car seats, cribs (unless you've checked it for recall and it adheres to current safety standards), and crib mattresses.

The Consumer Product Safety Commission post all recalls on their website. www.cpsc.gov/cpscpub/prerel/category/toy.html is for toy recalls. For all other children's items go to www.cpsc.gov/cpscpub/prerel/category/child.html.

Planning Ahead

The Family Medical Leave Act (FMLA) requires your employer to give you 12 weeks of unpaid leave and keep your position open for you. However, if your family is reliant on your income, this may not be feasible for you. The more you save up before your child is born, the longer you can afford not to work.

If your active-duty spouse is the mother, she will receive full pay for the time she is off work. This does not count against her leave allowance.

Ask the Chief

Most childcare services (including the Child Development Center) will not take babies younger than six weeks old.

What Is WIC and Do You Qualify?

WIC stands for Women, Infants, and Children. It is a Federal program to aid low-income families with nutritional needs for themselves and their children.

The income requirements past July 1, 2008 have not been released as of this writing. But you can view them at www.fns.usda.gov/wic/howtoapply/incomeguidelines.htm. Income is a factor, but there are others, such as nutritional need.

Most states don't include BAH, but some do (such as Colorado and Washington State). This can really make a difference in your income eligibility, so check with your local WIC office.

How the WIC Program Works

You will receive drafts (like checks) for certain items. These can be used at most grocery stores, including the Commissary. You are limited to certain brands that are nutritional (so don't expect to use your cereal check for chocolate cereal). Foods covered include cereal, infant formula, fruit juice, dairy (eggs, milk, cheese), dried beans/peas, peanut butter, and more.

The brand of infant formula depends on the state you live in. The Infant Formula Rebate System is a program to help keep costs down for the WIC State Agency. They sign a contract with one formula manufacturer to provide only that brand. In exchange, that manufacturer gives the WIC State Agency a rebate for every can of their formula a WIC participant gets. This helps to provide more money for the WIC program and enables the agency to help more people (literally millions more).

If your child has a specific dietary need, other formula brands can be provided so long as your pediatrician gives you a prescription for it.

You will meet with a nutritionist quarterly, and you will need to get weight and height measurements for your child quite regularly. This is for the nutritional part of the eligibility requirement to ensure that your child is growing properly.

> **Top's Tips**
>
> Even if you don't qualify for WIC, you might be able to get assistance if the formula is a medical necessity. If you are exclusively breastfeeding and forced to switch to a specific formula because of your child's allergies or other medical issues, talk to your pediatrician about the possibility of TRICARE covering the cost of the formula. Each region has different policies about this, but it's worth asking.

Locating Your Local WIC Office

You will usually find a local office within your military hospital. However, if your hospital doesn't have one, you can find an office at www.fns.usda.gov/wic/Contacts/statealpha.HTM.

If you are overseas, you can still qualify for WIC. It's called WIC Overseas. To determine if you are eligible, contact your local WIC office. The address and phone number is available at www.tricare.mil/mybenefit. Click Overview, then Special Programs, then Offices (under the Women, Infants, and Children Overseas heading at the bottom left of the page).

Overseas, they do not include housing allowances, COLA, or incentive pays in the income calculation, so you may qualify overseas even if you didn't within the States. Read the fact-sheet all about WIC and eligibility at www.fns.usda.gov/wic/WIC-Fact-Sheet.pdf.

Base Housing Upgrade

Base housing assignments are based on the number of family members in the household. Most bases have two bedroom units as the smallest available. That means if you have one child you will not get a bigger place. However, if you have two children, you will become eligible for a three-bedroom unit. These tend to be bigger all around.

Talk to your housing manager when you discover you are pregnant to see if there is a waiting list for the larger units. If so, get onto the list.

Most bases won't let you move if you're only recently pregnant because of the concern of miscarriage. However, if your area is short on two-bedroom units and has a lot of three bedrooms available, then you're more likely to get moved up quicker than if they're short of units all around.

The military will not pay to move you because it is not a PCS move. So, you'll need to rely on a rental truck and friends to help unless you want to pay for a moving company to do the work.

The Least You Need to Know

◆ When pregnant, it's your choice whether you want to be seen by your regular family practice doctor, or in the Obstetrics clinic. When delivering, it's whichever obstetrician is on duty in Labor and Delivery.

◆ Military hospitals offer many free classes that are beneficial for soon-to-be and new parents.

◆ Most childcare services require your child to be six weeks or older before they will accept him or her into their care.

◆ A child born overseas to a U.S. citizen parent is automatically a U.S. citizen, but the birth must be registered at the local U.S. consulate.

◆ To qualify for WIC you must meet both income and nutritional need requirements.

Chapter 6

Navigating the Childcare System

In This Chapter

- Childcare options (daycare, in-home, etc.)
- How to find the best childcare provider
- What it will cost you
- How to become an in-home childcare provider
- When you only want part-time or need evening/weekend care
- Who gets priority on the childcare waiting list

The military offers many child development programs. Unlike other benefits, the military is not required to offer subsidized childcare at every base, and spaces are limited, so not all eligible families will actually get a place.

Navigating the child development system can be frustrating, particularly if it's your first time doing it. There are quite a lot of hoops to jump through. But armed with the information in this chapter, you should find it a lot less confusing.

Child Development Centers

I mentioned Child Development Centers (CDC) in Chapter 3. They provide full-time daycare to children from six weeks to five years old. They also offer after-school programs for school-aged children up to age 12.

This is the most "daycare"-like of the child development services. The programs focus on childhood personal learning and educational development within a structured environment. Each CDC location must be accredited by both the Department of Defense (DoD) and the National Association for the Education of Young Children (NAEYC).

The opening hours are determined by your local center and are based on factors such as how far the CDC is from the base, typical working hours on that installation, etc.

Here's how to find the opening hours for your location:

1. Go to www.militaryinstallations.dod.mil.

2. Select Child Development Centers from the Program or Service menu (top left).

3. Enter your installation name or zip code.

4. Click Search.

5. Click the Child Development Center link in the listing on the left.

This will give you the address and phone number. Some listings show you the opening hours, too. If yours doesn't, just give them a call.

If there is no CDC nearby, you can run the search again for Child and Youth Registration and Referral. This department is responsible for helping military families find appropriate childcare in their local area.

Getting Registered

You can get the packet of paperwork to complete from the CDC itself. They can fax the completed forms to the Childcare Resource and Referral office for processing, or you can mail it in yourself.

You can also visit your Family Support Center. Most have a childcare referral office within them. This is where you register for non-CDC childcare programs, too.

How Much Will I Pay?

The amount is determined by your total household income (THI). It doesn't matter if you're married or not: if you live in the same home and share living expenses as a family unit, then both adult incomes are counted.

Some pays are included, others are not. A portion of your BAH is included, but not all of it. The CDC will calculate it.

The actual amount charged per fee category varies based on the cost of living in your location, but the THI ranges are set by the DoD, so you can at least see what category you are in. In my location, the fees range from $56 to $121 per week.

 **Top's Tips**

If you have to go onto the waiting list and your spouse is planning to deploy soon, you will need a specific Power of Attorney to accept the placement when one is available.

2008 Fees Categories for Military Childcare Services

Fee Category	THI range
1	under $28,000
2	$28,001–$34,000
3	$34,001–$44,000
4	$44,001–$55,000
5	$55,001–$70,000
6	$70,0001 and up

Go to your childcare services office (usually in the Family Support Center) and they can figure your cost for you before you fill out all of the paperwork. You'll need your spouse's most recent LES and your W2 (or last year's taxes if you're self-employed) to prove your income.

Hurry Up and Wait—The Priority Waiting List

Very few CDCs have immediate places available for all age ranges, so you will probably go onto the waiting list. This is not simply first-come-first-served. It's based on a priority order.

Priority 1: Dual active-duty parents, or single parents who are active-duty.

Priority 2: Active-duty parent with working or full-time student spouse (must be enrolled/working within 90 days of accepting placement).

Priority 3: Activated reservists or inactive on training.

Priority 4: DoD civilian contractors.

If you're at a base with three years remaining and you get pregnant, it's smart to get onto the waiting list immediately. That way you at least have a shot at getting a place for your child. Don't wait until you need the placement. The sooner you're on the list, the more likely you are to get the placement when you need it.

Many people stay on the list for a long time and then suddenly find a place opens up when their child turns two. This is not coincidence. The ratio of caregivers to children under two is much higher than for over two. Therefore there are far fewer under two placements, so the likelihood of getting a place dramatically increases after your child reaches two.

Family Child Care and Child Development Homes

There are only so many spaces in a CDC, and building an additional facility is often cost-prohibitive. So the alternative program is Family Child Care (FCC), or Child Development Homes (CDH) if you're Navy. These are licensed individuals who run a daycare from their home.

There are over 9,000 licensed FCC or CDH providers worldwide. The fee for full-time care is the same as the CDC if the child is under three. Over three years old, the provider sets the price. This is a great option for people who prefer home-based childcare. There is also much greater flexibility on hours for FCC and CDH. Many providers offer weekend and/or evening care. So if you work evenings and your spouse works on a rotating shift, you can still find care for your child.

The ratio is one adult to six children. Only two of those children may be under two years old. This includes the provider's own children.

There are strict standards the provider must adhere to. They begin with extensive training and background checks. Once their house passes the suitability inspection, they can begin accepting children. But, they do get surprise inspections once a month (more often if they're a new provider).

To find an FCC or CDH provider, visit your childcare services office. You will need to register for the program just like with the CDC. You may be offered a place with a specific provider, but you also have the option of calling around and interviewing providers from the list and then requesting a particular provider.

What to Look for When Interviewing a Provider

Trusting your child to someone else for any period of time can be hard. This makes the interview process even more important. Always interview a provider in person, in her home, with your child. You need to see the environment your child will be in, and how your child reacts to it. Also, the provider may act very different on the phone, or at a place outside her home.

The childcare services office suggests you look for certain things when interviewing a provider. I've added my own suggestions to this list too. At the end of the day your own instincts serve as your best indicator. It's quite normal to interview three or four providers before finding one you like.

Here's what to look for:

◆ Provider's home is clean and tidy.

◆ Organized toys and activities are around that can be reached by children.

◆ No safety hazards are present (uncovered plug outlets, glass doors that can be opened on cabinets, space heaters, etc.).

- Notice board is posted with up-to-date information about food menus, upcoming activities, etc.

- Food menu is nutritional and varied.

- Daily schedule has varied activities, and schedule is posted on the notice board.

- Provider interacts with your child and your child responds (may take a little while, but rapport should be established by the end of the interview).

- Your child seems happy in the environment and can't get into things she shouldn't have access to. (If the provider is saying "no, you can't have that" or is having to keep your child out of things, then the house is not adequately childproofed.)

- Look at the space available to the children. Often it is gated off from the rest of the house. Now imagine the number of children the provider will have in that space. If it seems very small, ask how she handles it without kids being in each other's pockets.

- Kitchen has cabinet locks on all doors, and chemicals are stored in a high cabinet (not under the sink, even if there is a child safety lock on the door).

- Each child has a "space" for his things (shoes, etc.).

- You agree with the provider's policy about items from home (some say no items from home, others recommend a favorite teddy for nap time, or something similar).

- If the provider has kids, watch them interact with your child. That can tell you more about the provider's style of childcare than any-thing she actually says.

- Ask for references and call them.

- Ask how she disciplines children and how that varies for each age she cares for.

- Ask how many children are in her daycare and how many she wants to have. A provider may only have three children in her care when you sign up with her, but within a month that group could double to six (maximum capacity).

◆ Listen to what the provider says. If she says her kids get sick a lot, you might wonder if it is something environmental. Even if it isn't, if her children are sick, the likelihood of your child catching it, or the daycare being closed, is much higher. These comments are often made off-hand, but pay attention to them.

◆ Ask how she handles a child with a cold at the daycare (toy sharing, allowed to be at daycare, etc.)

◆ Ask how she cleans the toys (it should be every evening, soaked in a bleach/water solution, rinsed, and then dried before the following day).

◆ Ask about her policy for unannounced parental visits. The answer should be that you're welcome any time, but to respect nap-time hours (which should be consistent and marked on the schedule).

◆ Ask how long the TV is on each day and what programs are watched. TV should be limited to under an hour total, and should not be on in the background during other activities.

◆ Go outside to look at the back yard. There should be some outdoor play time on the schedule, and the play area should be contained and tidy. Pets are not allowed around the children, but if the provider has a dog, you should also check that the backyard has been scooped recently, and that there are no holes or safety hazards that could affect your child when she's playing outside.

The provider should invite you to visit while she has the daycare children there, too. You should do this before you make a final decision, even if the interview went really well.

From Seasoned Spouses

If you talk to a provider who doesn't have a space, ask if she can recommend another provider. You can often find out about places that have not yet opened up. These placements are not on the list, so you may be able to reserve the spot before anyone else even knows it's becoming available.

Some providers charge a holding fee for placements opening in a month or two. The amount is not regulated through the FCC or CDH and may or may not be refunded if you do use the place you have reserved. My opinion is that providers shouldn't be making extra money for holding placements that do get used. If your provider charges a holding fee, make sure to get the details about cost and whether it is refunded before you pay anything (and always get a receipt).

If you don't like a provider or are not comfortable with her policies and way of doing things, *do not leave your child there*. It's as simple as that. You will be worrying the entire time you're apart from your child, and won't be able to function in the job you're trying to do (which is usually the reason for the childcare in the first place). It's better to take longer and interview lots of providers, so you know that whoever you select is definitely the right person for you.

What to Look for After Your Child Starts Daycare

The first few days, your child probably won't want to stay at daycare. It may take her a week or so to adjust. The provider should be used to this and able to distract your child.

After the first couple of weeks, your child should be settled and enjoy her time at daycare. You will have a two-week probationary period with the provider after which you decide if you want to continue. Your provider also has the option here to say that she doesn't want to continue caring for your child.

Watch for changes in your child's behavior or attitude. If she is becoming more aggressive, or defiant, you should ask the provider how she is at daycare. An unannounced drop-in might be useful to see how your child is interacting with the other kids.

Your provider should debrief you about the day. If you've got a very young child, you should get a sheet showing what she ate, how many wet and dirty diapers she had, how long she slept (and when), and her general behavior.

Most providers do craft activities with kids. So you should expect paintings and other crafts to come home with your child fairly regularly.

Keep an eye out for undocumented bumps and bruises. Kids get lots of bruises and you shouldn't be concerned about small ones, but if you notice a big bruise or cut, and the provider did not mention that your child hurt herself, you might want to ask about it the following day. You can request that if it happens again, that you be notified. That way, if it does happen again, she has no excuse for not telling you.

Becoming an FCC/CDH Provider

There are many benefits to becoming an in-home childcare provider, but it's not as easy as babysitting for a friend. There are strict regulations, training you must attend, background checks, reorganization of your house, paying for liability insurance, etc.

If you are interested in becoming an FCC or CDH provider, go to the childcare services office in your Family Support Center. They will have the application information and can explain all of the regulations and expectations of you (there are far too many to list here).

Drop-in or Part-Time Care

If you don't work full-time, then you probably don't want to pay for full-time care for your child.

The CDC doesn't usually offer regular part-time care because it is an inefficient use of the number of staff and spaces available. However, they do often offer drop-in care for spaces that are not filled for that particular day.

You have to be registered for drop-in care, but after that, you just call in the morning and see if they have a space for your child's age group. It's a first-come-first-served system; so if you want the space, you have to call early.

You'll find more drop-in spaces available during the school holidays, as more of the scheduled children will be on vacation.

Some bases have dedicated drop-in care centers. The difference here is that you can preregister your space even weeks in advance.

The main purpose of these drop-in centers is to provide care while you are at a medical appointment, or another appointment where you cannot take your child.

Both the CDC and drop-in centers charge $3 per hour, which is lower than many babysitters charge.

If you do book a space in the drop-in center for a nonmedical reason (to work out at the gym, to run errands, etc.) you could be bumped if someone who has a medical appointment needs that space. I used our local CDH drop-in center many times before I got regular care organized for my daughter. I wasn't bumped once. But then, I was also flexible with my timing.

The only downside I've found to the drop-in center is nap time. In our location there is only one room. So your child is still going to be around all the bigger kids who don't take naps.

If you work regular part-time hours, you may have a hard time finding childcare. Some FCC and CDH providers will take part-timers, but if your child is under two, it's very unlikely. This is because they only get the extra subsidy from the military if the child is full-time. Even two part-timers don't equal the amount they would get for one full-time placement.

Top's Tips

Even if you only want part-time care, go to your childcare office and have them calculate what you would pay for full-time. If you are in a lower price category, you might find it's not much more to pay for the full-time space than the $3-an-hour rate.

So, if you need regular part-time care, you may find you have to either pay for a full-time space or find civilian care.

It becomes less cost-effective to pay for a full-time space, the higher category you're in, but it may still be cheaper than part-time civilian care.

Finding Civilian Care

Talk to your local Department of Social Services or Department of Family and Protective Services to get a list of licensed off-base childcare providers in your area. You should also ask the licensing agency what a provider must do to become licensed. Some states have stricter regulations than others.

As regards civilian care, you often get what you pay for. Some daycare centers are very expensive, but the quality of care is high. If you're in the higher price categories for military childcare, it might not be much more (or could possibly be cheaper) for you to choose a civilian provider.

 From Seasoned Spouses

> When I was looking for daycare for my daughter, I discovered that it was only $50 more per month for full-time care at our local Montessori school than the CDC, because of the price category I was in.

Child Care Aware (www.childcareaware.org) is a website run by the National Child Care Resource and Referral Agencies (NCCRRA). It helps link parents with high-quality childcare services. Their Military Child Care In Your Neighborhood (MCCIYN) program is for active-duty families who cannot get a place in on-base care. They help match you with high-quality civilian childcare facilities that are accredited with one of these agencies:

◆ National Association for the Education of Young Children (NAEYC)

◆ National Accreditation Commission (NAC)

◆ National After-School Association (NAA)

◆ National Association of Family Child Care (NAFCC)

Alternatively, Family Child Care providers who have a Child Development Associate (CDA), Early Childhood Education, or Child Development degree are also permissible providers.

Because off-base care is often more expensive, there is also a military subsidy to help pay for the cost, so long as the provider meets the accreditation requirements. You can receive this subsidy for 60 days while you look for work, too, so you don't already have to have found your job. You can find out more at www.naccrra.org/MilitaryPrograms/program.php?Page=12.

Ask the Chief _____

Not all installations qualify for the MCCIYN program. To see if yours does, go to www.naccrra.org/MilitaryPrograms/progdesc.php or call 1-800-424-2246.

Operation Military Child Care is another program coordinated by NACCRRA to help with the cost of civilian childcare, but this one is specifically for while the military member is deployed.

Activated reserve and National Guard, and active-duty Army, Marine Corps, Air Force, and Navy who are deployed are eligible for the fee subsidy. You can receive it while your spouse is deployed, and for 60 days after he returns. You can also get this subsidy for 60 days while you try to find work. For more information, go to www.naccrra.org/MilitaryPrograms/program.php?Page=11.

The Least You Need to Know

- There are two main options for military childcare: Child Development Center (daycare facility) or Family Child Care (in-home care). You pay the same amount for both.

- The amount you pay for military childcare is based on your total household income.

- It can be very difficult to get a place for a child under two at the CDC because of the limited number of spaces.

- If you need evening and/or weekend care, you should look into Family Child Care/Child Development Homes.

- The waiting list for military childcare is not first-come-first-served. It is based on military priority.

- If there is no military childcare available, you may be eligible for a subsidy to help with the cost of high-quality civilian childcare.

Part 2

Moving in the Military

It happens to everyone, some more frequently than others—time to move. This part will help answer a lot of the questions about moving from one station to another, the allowances you will receive, how to settle in and find a new job, and what to expect if you move overseas.

7

The Dreaded PCS Move

In This Chapter

- ◆ Deciding whether to fly or drive
- ◆ Per diem and other travel allowances
- ◆ What is a DITY move and is it worth it?
- ◆ How to pass your housing inspection the first time
- ◆ Planning ahead for BAH differences

At some point in your military life, you will have to move. It might be 50 miles down the road, or across an ocean. Either way, you'll usually know about four to six months before the move.

This chapter will help you with the many decisions you'll have to make, and explain your various travel allowances.

To Fly or Not to Fly

Once your spouse has his or her written orders, you can start actually planning your Permanent Change of Station (PCS) move. This is different from a temporary duty (such as for training) or a deployment because the family is also moved.

The first decision you need to make is whether you want to fly or drive. If you fly, the military pays for your tickets. A moving company will pack up all of your household goods and transport them to the new location.

You will have the option of paying for additional insurance on the items (to cover replacement value rather than depreciated value), but if you have renter's insurance, you might be covered under that policy. Make sure to check so that you don't end up paying for the same insurance coverage twice.

It often takes a couple of weeks for your household goods to reach their destination (depending on where you're moving to and from). If you're flying, that means you're without your household goods for awhile after you arrive.

Some people ship essentials out on the day they depart so they will receive them within a couple of days. But that is not paid for by the military.

Flying is generally less hassle, but it also involves either an extended stay at a hotel, staying with family or friends, or staying in housing or a rental without most of your household items for a week or so.

Many Family Support Centers have Lending Lockers for furniture or other essential items for people who have not received their household goods yet. Call before you move to check if your Family Support Center has this, and what is usually available.

Transporting Pets

If you fly, you are responsible for the cost of shipping your pet. If you have a small pet, you may be able to bring her into the cabin and have her sit in a carrier beneath your seat. You will usually still pay a fee for this, but it's usually nicer for the animal than having her in the cargo area.

Most people with large pets moving within the States choose to drive rather than fly so they don't have pet shipping expenses.

Some airlines don't allow pets to be shipped during certain seasons where there is extreme hot or cold weather. You'll need to check with the airline about your departure and destination locations for the time of year you will be flying.

In Chapter 10 we'll look at how to transport a pet overseas.

Is It Worth Shipping a Vehicle?

If you are moving overseas, the military will pay to ship one vehicle for you. If you are moving within the States, you are responsible for all vehicle shipping fees and arrangements. If you want to keep your car, it might be better for at least one member of the family to drive, even if the others fly.

Typical vehicle shipping costs range from $350 to $1,500. Most shipping companies offer military rates, but you'll have to call to get that rate. You can get a list of shippers from your Personal Property or Transportation Office.

You might be able to get part of the cost covered by the military depending on various factors. To read more about this go to http://perdiem.hqda.pentagon.mil/perdiem/faqpov2pds.html.

Time for a Road Trip

You can generally make a bit of money if you drive, but if you're going from one coast to another and you've got kids or pets, that's a long journey.

My advice for long trips like this is to make it into a vacation. Visit family, or an interesting place that is somewhat on the route. It makes it fun for the kids and lets you visit places you wouldn't otherwise go to.

> **Top's Tips**
>
> Pick up a hotel chain location book so you can call ahead and book overnight accommodation when you know where you want to stop. If you book days in advance, you may feel pressured to go farther than you want if the weather's been bad or you're tired. Equally, if you get through that leg of the journey faster than anticipated, this enables you to push on for an extra hour or two rather than having to stop because you already booked your hotel for that night.

How Much Will Your Move Cost?

It really depends on the choices you make. If you fly, ship two vehicles, and you have a large pet to transport, you're going to pay a lot out-of-pocket. If you choose to drive with your pet in the back, you're not going to incur nearly as much extra cost.

Dislocation Allowance (DLA)

This is a perk many people forget about. It can be paid in advance so it really can help out if you do have additional expenses the military won't pay for.

The amount is based on your spouse's pay grade and whether the move is with or without dependents. The amount ranges from $784.23 for an E1 without dependents, to $3,931.50 for an O7 and above with dependents. The current rates can be found at http://perdiem.hqda.pentagon. mil/perdiem/dla.html.

Traveling Per Diem

You will receive *Per Diem* reimbursement for the days you are on the road. It is the Standard CONUS rate, which is $109 per day for fiscal year 2008.

Other people traveling with the sponsor (such as you and the kids) also get a Per Diem allowance.

Each dependent over 12 years old gets 75 percent of the Per Diem rate. $109 × 75% = $81.75.

def•i•ni•tion

> **Per Diem** literally means *per day* in Latin. In military terms it refers to a daily allowance for food, lodgings, and incidental expenses. It is paid during PCS travel, TDY/TAD, and deployments.

Children under 12 receive half of the Per Diem rate. $109 × 50% = $54.50.

So, if your family consists of you, your spouse, a nine-year-old, and a four-year-old, your total daily Per Diem would be:

$109 + $81.75 + $54.50 + $54.50 = $299.75

This includes lodging, meals, and incidental expenses.

To determine how many days you "need" for travel, the military looks at the *official distance* for the trip, and then divides that by 350 (in other words, you are expected to drive 350 miles per day). If the remainder is over 51 miles, they add one more day to your authorized travel time.

def•i•ni•tion

The military does not use what is on your odometer to calculate your mileage. They have an **official distance** for every trip. Unfortunately, you can't look up the distance yourself. Your Transportation or Personal Property Office should be able to tell you the mileage over the phone.

Mileage Allowance

If you drive your own vehicle, you will be paid 20 cents per mile for the official distance of your trip. This allowance is called Monetary Allowance in Lieu of Transportation (MALT). Our sample family of four would get $600 (3,000 miles × $0.20).

DITY Moves

A Do-It-Yourself, or DITY, move is when you arrange your household goods shipment yourself. There are three options:

- ◆ Hire a professional shipping company to do it all.

- ◆ Pack the goods yourself and have a shipping company transport them (also known as You-Pack-They-Drive).

- ◆ Pack and transport the goods yourself.

The first option is only really worthwhile if you can get a really good rate.

Packing your own goods can be a good option if you have time, but you'll need to get packing materials, boxes, etc. and plan for it to always take longer than you think. The third option adds procuring a vehicle to load into, driving the vehicle to the new duty station, unloading, and unpacking. This is a huge undertaking, and not one to take on lightly.

The plus side is that the military pays *you* instead of a shipping company. So, if it's just you and your spouse, this might be quite feasible. If you have kids and pets, this could be more of a challenge, and may be more hassle than it's worth.

Your first step is a visit to your Transportation or Personal Property Office. They will show you the forms you need to complete, as well as give you a list of ineligible items (such as house plants, pets, food, etc.) and let you know approximately how much you would receive (it's 95 percent of the rate they would pay a shipping company).

Partial DITY

Another option, most commonly used by people who drive to the new duty station, is a Partial DITY. This is exactly as it sounds. A professional shipping company will pack and transport most of your goods. But you pack some items and take them with you when you drive to the new duty station. You weigh the vehicle empty and then loaded, to show the weight you are carrying. You will be paid for that weight.

Most people do a Partial DITY move. It's a good way to make a little extra cash, and also ensures you have critical items with you as soon as you arrive at the new duty station.

Checking Out of Base Housing

You will need to complete a Notice of Intent to Vacate with the housing office. They will do a preliminary inspection to identify what you will need to do to pass the inspection.

How to Pass Your Housing Inspection the First Time

Because the housing representative who does your preinspection is usually the same person that does your final inspection, leaving a good impression the first time around is important. If he remembers that your unit was pretty good at preinspection, he's going to expect you to pass the final inspection.

Here are a few specific tips in addition to general cleaning (most of these were told to me during my preinspection when we moved out of housing last year):

◆ Wipe the tops and bottoms of all ceiling fan blades.

◆ Get new trays for the stovetop and have them sitting on the counter top (in packaging) for the preinspection. (Getting the new trays is a move-out requirement, but showing that you've done it already is a good thing.)

◆ Pull the stovetop up and clean under it.

◆ Run the self-clean cycle on the oven.

◆ Replace any burned-out bulbs (make sure to check under the stove, as these ones are easy to miss).

◆ Clean the vents above the stove.

◆ Wipe down the heating vents throughout your house.

◆ Clean the inside of the windows (outside are not your responsibility).

◆ Clean the tracks the windows sit in.

◆ Clean the baseboards.

◆ Clean the floor under and behind the fridge and oven.

◆ Clean and organize the inside of your fridge (yes, he will open it. An organized fridge says a lot about you).

◆ Tidy up the backyard and fill any holes dug by pets.

◆ Mow and edge the grass, and weed the flowerbeds.

◆ Spray a fresh, clean scent throughout the house before the inspection. Carpet refresher is a good option too (particularly if you have pets).

You are not expected to paint, but you are expected to clean the walls. If you've got crayon or black scuffmarks on the walls, I suggest you get those off even if you don't clean the entire wall before preinspection. I've found that Mr. Clean Magic Erasers are wonderful for getting stubborn marks off the walls.

You will need to redo some of these items before your final inspection, but it will be a lot easier to do the second time around, and I think it is well worth the effort.

For the preinspection, don't worry about cleaning the carpets. But you will have to have this done for your final inspection unless the carpets are scheduled to be replaced. Make sure to ask about this at the pre-inspection.

If the carpets won't be replaced, hiring a professional carpet cleaner is worth the money. In fact, some locations require a receipt showing that it was cleaned by a professional.

Hiring a Professional Cleaner

If you just don't want the hassle, you can hire a cleaner to stand the final inspection for you.

Your housing office will have a list of approved cleaners. The good part about this is that you stand a hand-over inspection, where the cleaner agrees to take responsibility for the cleaning of the house. You're free to leave at that point.

You will still be responsible for certain items, including cleaning behind the stove and fridge, getting replacement stove drip trays, replacing lightbulbs, etc., but all of these items will be on the list your housing office will give you.

> **Top's Tips**
>
> The cleaner's quote will be based on the condition of your house. So the cleaner it is when they visit, the lower the charge.

Get multiple quotes, they will vary. So long as the cleaner is on the approved list, it doesn't matter who you choose, so I recommend just finding the cheapest and booking early.

If you stand your own inspection and fail the first one, they will reschedule you for another inspection in a few days. If you've got plane tickets or travel plans fixed, this could force you to hire a cleaner anyway. If you fail the second time, they usually require you to get a professional cleaner in.

Waiting Lists for Base Housing

There may be a waiting list for housing at your new base. This could be a week or a few months. Once you get your orders, call ahead to the housing office in your new location and ask what the waiting list is like for the type of unit you will be assigned. Ask if you can be placed on the list in advance.

They will not hold a unit for you, but once you get to the new location, your wait should be much shorter than if you waited to apply until you got there.

Planning for the Budget Change

When you move, you may see a pay increase or decrease because of different incentive pays, and BAH rate changes. Once you know where you're going, it's very easy to look up the new BAH rate at http://perdiem.hqda.pentagon.mil/perdiem/bah.html.

If your spouse checks into the new command in December, you are entitled to the current year's rate. If the rate drops on January first, you are grandfathered in with the old rate, even though you just got there. If the BAH rate goes up, you get the higher amount, just like everyone else at that base.

Preparing Your Kids for the PCS

Moving is tough for kids. They're leaving their friends and everything that is familiar to them. It's important not to forget them when you're planning your PCS move. Making it into a vacation will help. Also, go to your new base's website and plan some events with your child that he can get excited about.

Having an Old Friend Come to Stay

Consider having a close friend of your child's visit a few months after you move. This way, your child can introduce her old friend to all of her new friends. This brings her two "worlds" together. By waiting a few months, you're letting her settle in, but also giving her something to look forward to.

I strongly suggest you do not let your child visit friends back at the old location, at least not for a while. A friend of mine let her 14-year-old daughter go back to see her friends during the summer after their move. It was a disaster. Her daughter didn't want to come back, and caused a lot of fuss because she hadn't fully transitioned into the new location yet.

Checking Graduation Requirements

High school graduation requirements vary by state and it's highly possible that your child could be a senior, on track to graduation in one state, but not meet the requirements in another. The Military Child Education Coalition has a website where you can find the education requirements for each state. Go to www.militarychild.org/ARC.asp, select your state, and Graduation/Promotion Requirements from the menu.

At the end of the day, PCSing is going to be hard for your kids. They will need a lot of support. The more planning you can do to prepare them for the move, the better.

The Least You Need to Know

◆ Flying is usually less hassle, but you'll have to wait for your household goods to arrive, and you'll have to ship your pets and vehicle at your own expense.

◆ Dislocation Allowance (DLA) helps cover expenses not otherwise covered by the military.

◆ You can opt to move your household goods yourself in a DITY move, or only move essentials in a Partial DITY move. Either way, you get paid for doing it.

◆ MALT (mileage allowance) is paid for the official distance of your move—not what shows on your odometer.

◆ Check graduation requirements ahead of time for kids in high school.

Chapter 8

Your New Permanent Duty Station

In This Chapter

- ◆ Calculating and maximizing your TLE allowance
- ◆ When your spouse is eligible for house-hunting leave
- ◆ Finding off-base housing
- ◆ The Military Clause

You made it! You're at your new duty station. Now you need to begin the process of settling in. This starts with finding a place to live.

There are some other allowances available to you once you arrive at your new station, both in terms of free leave and actual monetary reimbursement. In this chapter, we will look at both of these benefits, as well as housing options, what to look for in your lease, and the all-important Military Clause.

Temporary Accommodation

Unless you or your spouse were able to visit ahead of time and secure a home, you will need to stay in temporary lodgings until you can find a permanent place to live.

The military will pay for 10 days of living expenses for you, which they consider to be ample time for you to find a place. This allowance is called your Temporary Lodging Expense (TLE). It is different from your travel Per Diem, and the amount paid is based on your duty station zip code.

TLE can be used before you leave your old duty station, when you arrive at your new location, or a combination of both. However you choose to split it up, the maximum is 10 days. If you are moving overseas, you can only use five days of TLE before you move. However, there is another allowance, called TLA (Temporary Lodging Allowance), which covers you at the other end of the journey for a much longer period of time (see Chapter 10).

Calculating your TLE may seem intimidating, but it's not actually that complicated. Your spouse can ask his finance admin for assistance if this really doesn't make sense to you.

Per Diem Rates

The first thing you need to do is find the local Per Diem rate. While you were traveling, you received the Standard CONUS Per Diem rate. This changes once you reach your destination. Now it is calculated based on zip code. To find your area's rate, go to http://perdiem.hqda. pentagon.mil/perdiem/perdiemrates.html.

Select your state from the box on the left (marked Contiguous United States) and then click Execute.

You'll see a table showing all city locations near bases within that state. To make this clearer, I've reproduced the table showing my location, Oak Harbor, Washington.

Local Per Diem Rates for Oak Harbor, WA (for fiscal year 2008)

Location	County	Season	Max. Lodging	Local Meals	Prop. Meals	Incidentals	Maximum Per Diem	Effective Date
OAK HARBOR	ISLAND	06/01-08/31	94	56	33	3	153	10/1/2007
OAK HARBOR	ISLAND	09/01-09/30	80	56	33	3	139	10/1/2007
OAK HARBOR	ISLAND	10/01-05/31	80	56	33	3	139	10/1/2007

There is far more information in this table than you really need to calculate TLE; however, I've included all of it, as this is what the website shows.

You'll notice that there are three rows for this location. This is because the lodging rate changes, based on the season. If your location has more than one rate, make sure to look at the Season column to make sure you're looking at the correct rates.

Calculating Your TLE

Now that you have your Per Diem table handy, the first thing you need to calculate is your *M&IE* rate. Simply add the amounts in the Local Meals and Incidentals columns. Always ignore the Prop. Meals column; this doesn't apply to you.

def•i•ni•tion

Meals and Incidental Expenses (or **M&IE**) is the total of the Local Meals and Incidentals allowances.

The Local Meals rate for Oak Harbor is $56 and the Incidentals rate is $3. This gives us an M&IE rate of $59.

Now you need to calculate the percentage of the lodging and M&IE rates that apply to you and your family. This is based on the number of dependents staying in the hotel and their ages. If there are more people traveling together than just you and your spouse, the percentage is going to be over 100 because you add the percentage allowance for each additional dependent. This is very similar to how you calculated your travel Per Diem.

Percentage of Lodging and M&IE Rates Allowed for Each Member of Your Family

Persons Eligible for TLE Allowance	Percentage of Rate Allowed
Active-duty alone	65%
Active-duty military *plus* one dependent (i.e., you)	100%
Each additional dependent under 12	25%
Each additional dependent over 12	35%

You could calculate each person's rate separately and then add them together, but I find it easier to work out the total percentage allowed and then just do the calculations once.

Let's work through a full example.

Let's say you, your spouse, and your toddler stay in a hotel in Oak Harbor for 10 nights from July 15 to July 25. The 125 percent rate applies for you (100 percent for you and your spouse, plus 25 percent for your toddler).

The maximum lodging rate for this season in Oak Harbor is $94. This is the 100 percent rate. Because your family is eligible for 125 percent of the rate, simply multiply $94 by 125 percent (94 × 1.25) to get your total daily lodging allowance of $117.50. Now you need to do the same thing with the M&IE rate.

You already determined the M&IE rate is $59 (by adding the Local Meals and Incidental columns). So multiply $59 by 125 percent (59 × 1.25), to get a maximum M&IE rate of $73.75 per day.

You may think that you can spend $191.25 on lodging and meals ($117.50 + $73.75), but there is one more thing to take into account ....
The maximum TLE allowance for your entire family is $180 per day (no matter where you are stationed).

So you will only receive $180 even though the calculations suggest you should get $11.25 more than that. To have the full expense covered by TLE, you need to spend $11.25 less on your hotel or food per night.

Fire in the Hole!

The maximum daily payment for TLE is $180 for your whole family. Even if your combined percentage allowances take you well over that, you will only receive $180 per day.

Common TLE Calculation Errors That Can Cost You Hundreds

When people calculate that they will go over the maximum TLE rate, most automatically reduce the lodging expense and then assume the remainder up to $180 can be used for food or incidentals. This is not necessarily the case.

When the TLE payment is calculated on your travel claim, your actual lodging expense (including tax) will be compared against the maximum allowance, and the *lower of the two* will be paid.

Let's keep working with the Oak Harbor example. If you spend the maximum allowances ($117.50 lodging and $73.75 M&IE), you exceed the $180 daily cap. So you decide to stay at a cheaper hotel and only spend $70 per night on lodging. $180 − $70 = $110, so that's what you can spend on food and incidentals, right? Wrong.

TLE will pay your *exact lodging expense* up to $117.50 per night. So, if you spend $70, you will only be reimbursed for $70. Your M&IE rate is $73.75 and that will not increase, even if you spend less on your lodging. So your daily TLE payment would actually be $70 (lodging) + $73.75 (M&IE) = $143.75.

This is where you can easily find yourself out of pocket on your travel claim reimbursement. If you assumed you would still be getting $180 per day for 10 days, you'd expect to receive $1800. However, you would actually receive $1,437.50 ($143.75 × 10 days). That $36.25 per day calculation error means you would receive $362.50 less on your travel claim than you expected. That's a lot, particularly if you've already spent it!

Now, let's look at how you can avoid this happening.

Maximizing the TLE Allowance

Most people don't need the full allowance for M&IE, but that means if you plan wisely, you can actually make a bit of money from this.

Let's continue with our Oak Harbor example. If your actual lodging expense is $117.50, then your M&IE is reduced to $62.50 (to keep you under the $180 cap). To maximize the allowance, you want to get the full M&IE rate. So subtract the maximum M&IE from the $180 cap. $180 − $73.75 = $106.25.

This $106.25 is the maximum you should spend on lodging (including tax). You can go lower, but remember that your M&IE won't go any higher (as you can see in the following table).

TLE payment breakdown based on actual lodging expenses using figures for Oak Harbor, WA

Actual Lodging Expense (inc. tax)	M&IE Paid	Total Daily TLE Paid
$117.50	$62.50	$180.00
$110.00	$70.00	$180.00
$106.25	$73.75	$180.00
$90.00	$73.75	$163.75
$70.00	$73.75	$143.75
$50.00	$73.75	$123.75

You gain nothing by staying in a hotel under $106.25 per night, so stay in the nicest place you can find up to that amount.

Now, let's look at how much you can make if you don't actually use the full M&IE allowance.

Let's say you only actually spent $40 on food. That's $33.75 less than the maximum allowance, or $337.50 over 10 days. That extra is yours to keep.

Remember, these numbers are based on the rates we calculated for Oak Harbor, Washington. You will need to look up the rates for your location and run these calculations for yourself to see how much you can spend and make.

Top's Tips

Make sure you include the hotel tax (if they charge it to military guests) when comparing hotel rates to your maximum lodging allowance. Also, if you're staying at your departing duty station for a few nights, and then at the new duty station for the remainder, you will need to run the calculations for both locations. Your TLE will be different for each part of your stay based on where you are that night.

Staying with Family

If you're lucky enough to have family in the area you are moving to, you may choose to stay with them before you find a place to live, rather than stay in a hotel. What most people don't realize is that you're still eligible for TLE even if you stay with family. You are not eligible for the lodging allowance part, but you are eligible for M&IE (which is one reason why they calculate them separately).

Using the Oak Harbor example, if you stayed with family for 10 days before finding a home, you would be eligible for $73.75 per day for M&IE. Over 10 days, that's $737.50. Most people don't realize they are eligible for this, so they never claim it.

Waiting For Government Housing

In Chapter 7 I suggested you place your name on the base housing waiting list at your new station before you PCSed, if you wanted to go into government housing. If you did that, great! You are one step closer to getting your new home. If not, this should be one of your first priorities when you get to the new base.

If there is no waiting list for base housing, you must go straight into housing rather than using TLE. There are a few exceptions (such as if your household goods have not yet arrived) but in general, you are expected to go straight into government quarters if they are available. Having said that, rarely is there immediate availability for housing.

If nothing is available yet, but you do want to go into government housing once a unit opens up, you should talk to your housing representative about short-term rentals in the area. They're usually a bit more expensive, but don't require a year lease. Most of the time, you can find a short-term rental for three or six months.

If it's just you and your spouse, it might be cheaper and less hassle to hold off on receiving your household goods and stay in a hotel or a fully furnished place that offers weekly or monthly rates until a place opens up in base housing.

If you go this route, let the Travel Management/Personal Property Office know that you want your shipment to go into storage. You can leave it there for up to 60 days; after that you will need special permission for an extension, or pay for the extra storage time yourself.

If you need your household goods immediately, or if the waiting list is over four months, you might consider looking for proper off-base lodging in the meantime.

Many rental agreements include a Military Clause, which will allow you to break the lease if you are offered and accept a place in government housing (I'll talk about this more in a moment). Call around the local rental agencies and ask if they have a Military Clause in their contract and what it covers.

How BAH Rates Are Calculated

Your housing allowance is based on three things: your spouse's rank, the location you live in, and whether he is eligible for with or without dependents. If you're married, or he has custody of a child from a previous marriage, he will get the with dependents rate. You can find your BAH rate at http://perdiem.hqda.pentagon.mil/perdiem/bah.html.

The BAH rate is supposed to cover most of your household expenses (rent and utilities). I know many seasoned spouses are laughing at that. For many people it seems that BAH doesn't even come close to covering utilities as well as rent.

This is generally because the BAH rate for each rank is also linked to specific types of housing. For example, an E5 with dependents gets BAH based on renting a two-bedroom townhouse. It doesn't matter if that E5 has three children. The rate is the same whether he has one dependent or five.

Many people choose to go into government housing simply because of this. If you need more bedrooms than your BAH accounts for, you will get a better place in base housing than off-base. This is because government-housing units are assigned based on number of rooms needed. So the E5 with a spouse and three children will get a four-bedroom unit.

Locating Off-Base Housing

If you're looking for off-base housing, a trip to your housing office is still very worthwhile. They are like a hub for all local rental agencies and individuals wanting to rent their property directly to military families.

The housing representative can print you a list of all rental properties in the area and restrict the results to match your specific needs. You can specify certain search criteria such as distance from the base, price range, type of accommodations (house, condo, apartment, etc.), pet rules, and the number of bedrooms/bathrooms.

The list isn't always completely up to date, but it's still a huge timesaver, because you don't have to bother calling about properties that clearly don't meet your needs, going to rental agencies that don't manage properties in your price range, or don't allow pets if you have one.

House-Hunting Leave

Your spouse is eligible for 10 days of *Permissive TDY* for house-hunting leave.

def•i•ni•tion

Permissive TDY (TAD for Navy/Marine Corps) gives a military member time off that is not charged to his leave balance. It is used in many circumstances, one of which is to give a military member (with a family) time to look for a home during a PCS move.

Most of the time you'll hear Permissive TDY referred to as "No-cost TDY." As much as I would love the "no cost" part to mean "no cost to you," it really means the exact opposite. It means no cost to the military. Your spouse will not have the time charged to his leave balance, which is good, but any expenses incurred during house-hunting leave (flights, accommodations, etc.) are solely your responsibility.

Most people time it so they arrive at their new duty station at least 10 days before the report-no-later-than date (on your spouse's orders). This means you can take house-hunting leave to coincide with the

10 days TLE will pay for you to stay in a hotel. This way you don't incur any general-living expenses during the house-hunting leave period.

The Military Clause

No, this is not Santa dressed up in camouflage (although that does conjure an interesting image). It is a "get out" clause in your rental contract for certain specific circumstances.

You should never sign a lease that doesn't have a Military Clause in it. The *Servicemembers Civil Relief Act (SCRA)* gives you the power to break a lease only under very specific circumstances. A Military Clause covers far more eventualities.

def•i•ni•tion_____

> The **Servicemembers Civil Relief Act** of 2003 (the rewrite of the Soldiers and Sailors Act of 1940) gives you the ability to break a lease that was signed prior to becoming active-duty (for example, if your spouse was a reservist and then was activated, or was a civilian and then joined the military). It also allows you to break a lease if you are given PCS orders. But it doesn't give any provisions for if you are waiting for government housing, or other scenarios you may face.

Many states already have a statewide Military Clause that protects military families; however, it is always smart to have terms specifically outlined in your lease anyway.

You can add a Military Clause to your lease as an addendum (with the landlord's permission) if it is not already included. Each state has different requirements, so get the wording from your legal office on base. It's always smart to have them read your lease before you sign it anyway.

Assuming you have a Military Clause in your rental contract, and you are offered government housing, you only need to give your landlord 30 days' written notice (or whatever is specified in the Military Clause) that you will be moving, even if it is only 2 or 3 months into your 12-month lease. You should get your deposit back (minus any damages).

The military will not move your household goods again. It will be up to you to move your household goods from your current location if you choose to accept the place in government housing. However, if you had your household goods placed in storage and are currently renting a furnished home, the military will pay to have the goods brought out of storage and delivered to your new home.

The Least You Need to Know

- ◆ Calculate your TLE before you PCS so you know exactly how much you can spend once you get to your destination.

- ◆ You can make a bit of money if you budget your lodging and food expenses wisely.

- ◆ TLE is paid for a maximum of 10 days for CONUS moves, and 5 days if you are moving overseas.

- ◆ Permissive TDY/TAD gives you 10 days of free leave to search for a new home.

- ◆ Insist on a Military Clause in any rental contract you sign, and get the legal office to look over the lease before you sign it.

Chapter 9

Settling In and Getting Connected

In This Chapter

- ◆ Do you qualify for unemployment compensation?
- ◆ Getting a new job
- ◆ Building your "Mom Network"
- ◆ Getting your kids in school

If you've relied on your full-time income in your budget, PCSing is a scary time. The objective is to find another job quickly, but the local economy will determine what you will get paid for a similar job (and even if there are jobs available).

During a PCS move a few years back, I left a job making $15 an hour to move to an area where the same job paid about half that. I settled at a job paying $8.50 an hour, which was good for that area. In the space of just a few weeks, my income dropped from about $30,000 a year to $16,000. That meant $1,150 per month less for our budget.

My move caught me off guard. We hadn't planned on losing that much income considering I was doing the same type of job and hours. The cost of living was a bit lower, but static expenses like car payments don't change when you move. In fact, our insurance went up because we moved into a hurricane-prone area.

The moral of this story is to do your research ahead of time. Look at www.monster.com or www.careerbuilder.com for jobs, as soon as your spouse knows where the new orders will be. This will give you an idea of the general pay scale. That way, you can begin adjusting your budget months in advance, so you won't have a huge shock when you get there.

Unemployment Compensation for Transferred Spouses

Leaving your job when you PCS is not a choice; it's a necessity. There are 21 states that understand this and will give you unemployment compensation while you search for a new job.

Some states offer this to all spouses who relocate because of their spouses' job, whether or not they are in the military (called Transferred Spouse Exception), while others are only for military spouses (called Military Spouse Exception). Either way, if you move to one of these 21 states, you are eligible for unemployment compensation so long as you are seeking work.

Those 21 states are Arizona, Arkansas, California, Connecticut, Florida, Georgia, Indiana, Kansas, Maine, Montana, Nebraska, Nevada, New Jersey, New Mexico, North Carolina, Oklahoma, Pennsylvania, Rhode Island, South Carolina, Texas, and Washington.

There are eight states that specifically exclude spouses from receiving unemployed compensation based on their spouse's job transfer. They consider it a "voluntary quit" even if you are transferred because of military service. These states are Colorado, Maryland, North Dakota, Ohio, South Dakota, Utah, Vermont, and Virginia.

All other states offer unemployment compensation on a case-by-case basis, or have a waiting period before you become eligible. Remember, it is the state you transfer *to*, not *from*, that must offer the coverage for you to be eligible.

From Seasoned Spouses

> Military spouses are a prideful bunch, and we like to think we can do everything without help from anyone else. If you don't need the extra income, then don't apply for unemployment compensation. However, if you're barely making ends meet after your move, this is a program that is there to assist you. You may only need it for a couple of weeks, but those few extra hundred dollars can mean a lot in the finances of a military family.

At www.usa4militaryfamilies.dod.mil you can see the progress of the campaign to get all states to provide unemployment compensation to all transferred military spouses.

Careers for Military Spouses

Yes, I know the concept of a "career" might sound crazy. It's hard for a military spouse to find a job that transfers enough to make it into a career.

I work from home, which is great from a PCSing point of view, but it does have its challenges regarding time-management and separation of work and home. Still, I think work-from-home jobs are a great option for military spouses.

You'll see scams all over the Internet with "work-from-home opportunities" in which you can't really make any money, but among them there are some legitimate jobs.

Selling Items on eBay

I'm sure there's a meeting somewhere where I should stand up and say, "Hi, my name is Lissa McGrath, and I'm addicted to eBay." I really am. I've been active on eBay since 1999, and I still love buying and selling on there. This is something that any military spouse can do. When you get ready to PCS, sell your extra stuff on eBay rather than at a yard sale. It will take you about the same amount of time to set it all up, and you'll make far more money. Anything left over can be yard-saled, or given to charity and the value deducted on your taxes.

I've helped many military friends learn about eBay. Some use it to supplement their income; others really get into it and become full-time sellers. Your buyers don't care if you're in Maine, Mississippi, or Montana; they're paying for shipping anyway.

I wrote a book about eBay last year, and I can't even begin to condense it all into one chapter. If you are interested in making a full-time, part-time, or just occasional income on eBay, please consider reading either my book (*The Complete Idiot's Guide to eBay*) or another book on the topic, to get familiar with the ins and outs of eBay before you get started.

Creating Your Own Product and Website

There are many spouses who create products tailored to other military families and sell them on their own website as well as eBay and Amazon. If you've got some creative ideas and skills, why not try it?

Military-Friendly Companies

Employers cannot discriminate against you because you are a military spouse. In fact, they are not allowed to ask you outright if you are a military spouse. However, they can ask questions like, "Why does your resumé show you have moved around a lot?" or "What brings you to this area?" which are very difficult to answer without disclosing your military link.

Some companies don't want to employ military spouses, because we are almost guaranteed to quit within three or four years. In companies where most people stay for 10 to 15 years, this is considered a waste of training and development resources.

Don't be discouraged. While there are companies who don't wish to employ military spouses, others welcome us with open arms. Those who know about military spouses know that we work hard, we can handle stress and multitasking with ease, we don't need health-care insurance or other benefits like that, and we are adaptable to new situations.

Some nationwide companies specifically recruit military spouses. Their military programs allow spouses to transfer between stores when they move. So, you're doing the same job with the same company, just in a different location. This gives you the opportunity to advance in your own career with the same company, even though you are moving every few years.

Military Spouse magazine created a top-10 list of military-friendly companies for 2007 (out of 2500 major companies). The article goes into detail about each company and why it was picked. It can be read at www.milspouse.com/uploadedFiles/site_components/MSM.Top10.pdf. For future years, look for a link on www.milspouse.com.

Here are the results:

1. USAA   www.usaa.apply2jobs.com/veterans_and_military_spouses.htm

2. AAFES   http://odin.aafes.com/employment

3. RE/MAX   www.remax.com/inside_remax/become_an_agent/operation_remax/index.aspx

4. The Home Depot   https://careers.homedepot.com/cg/content.do?p=military

5. Wachovia   www.wachovia.com/careers

6. Computer Sciences Corporation (CSC)   www.csc.com/careers

7. Sears Holdings Corporation   http://searsholdings.com/careers/military

8. Kelly Services   www.kellyservices.us/military

9. Lockheed Martin   www.lockheedmartinjobs.com

10. Starbucks   www.starbucks.com/careers

Military.com has an interesting search feature that enables you to search by the base where you are going to be stationed. Go to www.military.com/spouse and click Search Jobs By Installation.

Military.com also has a long list of military-spouse-friendly companies at www.military.com/spouse/0,,employer_list,00.html.

Assistance from Your Family Support Center

In Chapter 4 I talked about your Family Support Center. One of the programs I mentioned was the Family Employment Readiness Program (FERP). This used to be called the Spouse Employment Assistance Program (SEAP), and some bases may still use that name. The FERP office has career counselors on staff who will help you work on your resumé and job applications, provide lists of jobs in the area, help you with interview techniques, etc. These are usually the same people who run the TAP (Transition Assistance Program) for active-duty members who are retiring or getting out of the military. So, they really know what they're talking about.

Connecting with Other Spouses

One of the important steps of settling in at a new unit or command is meeting other spouses and making friends. It may seem hard at first; after all, you've left your good friends behind at your old duty station. But, with a little effort and an open mind you can make great friends anywhere.

From Seasoned Spouses

If you have young kids, it's quite easy to meet other families. I go for a walk with my daughter in her stroller most evenings. This is a great way to meet other moms with kids around the same age as yours. Also, check out the programs at your on-base gym. We have Toddlercise, which is 30 minutes of music and dance for parents and toddlers from one to three years old. They also have a "Stroller Strut" program twice a week for moms to meet and go walking together. Both of these programs are a great way to meet new people.

There are many "Mom" groups, playgroups, etc. around each base. If you're having a tough time finding them, ask a nurse at Pediatrics (they'll usually have flyers) or give your Family Support Center a call.

I think networking is hardest on spouses without kids. When we first moved to a deploying command (before our daughter was born), I felt completely set apart from everyone else. At command functions, all the spouses with kids knew each other and, even though I knew them, too, it wasn't the same kind of friendship. We didn't do things together outside of command functions.

If you're in this situation, consider getting involved in local community events. Boys and Girls Clubs of America are always looking for volunteers, as are local schools. Find out about organizations in your area and get involved. It's a whole lot better than sitting at home on your own while your spouse is gone. You'll find that many other spouses get involved in these organizations, and it's a great way to meet people and find a way into established friendship circles.

Another great networking place is your command's FRG (Family Readiness Group). They organize various events for spouses (including "over the hump" parties for deployed commands) and usually have regular meetings. They should know about small groups that meet without kids (lunch/coffee groups, etc.), too.

Enlisted/Officer's Spouse Organizations

Sometimes these are called wives clubs, but more often now is the more PC "spouse organization." Yes, some can be catty and full of gossip, but others are great networking groups that do a lot for the community as well as supporting each other during difficult times.

You can be as active as you like in these groups. Some people really get into it, while others attend meetings and help out at events but don't want a "leadership" role. Either way, you'll most likely find at least a few people who are similar to you.

Getting Your Kids Enrolled in School

Once you've found a place to live, you'll know what school district you are in. You may have only one elementary, middle, or high school in your city, or there may be multiple schools for each age range. If you're choosing a state-run school, there's not much involved other than calling the applicable school and setting up a time to register. You may have already done this in your pre-PCS planning. If so, the transition should be fairly smooth.

If you have a choice of schools, ask your spouse to get recommendations from other families in your command.

The important thing is to get your child registered as soon as possible if he or she is missing school because of your move. If nothing else, it will help your child get into a routine, which helps with the settling-in process. Being the new kid is tough, but it's just as important for your kids to make new friends as it is for you to do so.

When you're stationed overseas, there are different choices and challenges to your child's education. We will address all of this in Chapter 10.

The Least You Need to Know

- ◆ Look at comparable jobs in your new area before you PCS, so if there is to be a decrease in pay it doesn't come as a shock.

- ◆ If your state allows it, consider applying for unemployment compensation until you find a new job.

- ◆ There are many military-spouse-friendly companies that will let you transfer your job when you PCS so you can work on a "career" rather than a series of "jobs."

- ◆ Get out there and meet people. It will make settling in much swifter for you and your family.

- ◆ Get your kid enrolled in school as soon as possible. Playing catch-up is not a good way to start a new school.

Chapter 10

Moving and Living Overseas

In This Chapter

- ◆ Important household good and vehicle shipping information
- ◆ Getting an overseas driver's license
- ◆ Programs exclusive to overseas families
- ◆ Choosing between the DoD and local community school
- ◆ TRICARE overseas
- ◆ Helping your kids prepare for the move

Moving overseas is like nothing you've done before. There are different logistics as well as benefits and financial allowances that apply when you move overseas versus within the United States. In some cases, Alaska and Hawaii are considered overseas because they're not attached by land to the rest of the United States.

Shipping Your Household Goods

When you move overseas you will be without your household goods for awhile (maybe months). So, you need to pack efficiently.

Types of Shipments

Because you have to fly to your new station, you don't have the option of a DITY or Partial DITY move to take essential items, so you get two household goods shipments instead of just one. The first is for essentials (linens, flatware, clothing, etc.) and goes by air. It is called *Unaccompanied Baggage (UB)*. The rest of your household goods go in a second shipment by ship.

def•i•ni•tion

Unaccompanied Baggage (UB) is available for all branches of the service. This is for essentials only. The only type of furniture allowed is flat-packed baby furniture.

The allowance for UB is determined by the military member's rank, branch of service, and the destination. There is a smaller additional allowance for each family member. The amount of the UB allowance that you actually use is deducted from your total household goods allowance, it is not an additional allowance.

Vehicle Shipping

The military will usually ship one vehicle for your family's use overseas (called a *concession vehicle*). If you have a leased vehicle (or are still making payments on a purchased vehicle), you can still take it, provided you meet certain criteria.

def•i•ni•tion

Concession vehicle means a vehicle you have not paid local tax on (i.e. in the country you're now stationed in). This could be a vehicle you've purchased tax-free within the country, or imported from the United States (whether or not you paid sales tax on it), or bought from another U.S. servicemember at the overseas base.

There must be 12 months or more left on your lease agreement, and you must get written permission from the leaseholder. If you still have a lien on the vehicle, the lien-holder (your bank usually) will have to provide written permission for you to take it out of the country.

Once your vehicle has been shipped, you can track it through www.whereismypov.com using the order number on your DD 788 form.

There is a really useful PDF document available at www.sddc.army.mil/sddc/Content/Pub/8808/DBCN8808.pdf, which covers a lot of the little details about shipping a vehicle. On page 13 and 14 of the document you'll find the address, phone number, and opening hours for all of the Vehicle Processing Office locations both CONUS and OCONUS. You have to deliver your vehicle to one of these offices to be processed so check where your closest one is.

You are limited on the number of concession vehicles you can have at any one time. For a single person, it is always one. For a family, it's usually two vehicles. You can usually have more vehicles, but you will have to pay local tax on them. So if you buy a vehicle *on the economy*, you will pay whatever tax that country charges for that vehicle.

> **def•i•ni•tion**
>
> Buying something **on the economy** means buying it off-base in the local currency. You will also pay the local taxes on the item (which can be very high).

Many people take one vehicle with them and then purchase another at the new location. Many bases have on-base vehicle lots, and most also have rental vehicles available for decent rates so you don't have to be without a car while you get settled in.

Overseas Driver's License

You will need a permit to drive in the country you are stationed in. Each country has different requirements. Usually it is a written test that is administered at the Vehicle Registration Office (VRO), but there may be a practical component as well. You'll get information about this at your newcomer's brief.

Insurance

Check if your vehicle insurance company offers coverage for overseas military. If not, you will have to choose to either switch to a U.S.-based company that does, or pay for insurance from a company in the country you are transferring to.

You will need to arrange for vehicle licensing in the country you're going to be living in. Again, you can get this information at your Vehicle Registration Office.

Arriving at the Base

Always attend the Newcomer's Brief (it may be called Indoc or Welcome Brief). This covers lots of information about living in that country, and also information specific to that base. When you plan to leave an overseas base, you should attend the Smart Moves brief. I suggest both you and your spouse attend, because there's a lot of information passed out that you won't get elsewhere. I can't stress enough, how important attending the briefs for arriving and departing an overseas base are.

Overseas Allowances

There's no beating around the bush—moving overseas is stressful. But, thankfully, the military does give you extra financial allowances to help with that particular strain. Some of them you know already, just by a different name. Others are only for military families living overseas.

Temporary Lodging Allowance (TLA)

We talked about TLE (Temporary Lodging Expense) in Chapter 8. TLA (Temporary Lodging Allowance) is basically the same, just for overseas moves. You are authorized TLE for five days before you depart the United States, then you are usually authorized TLA once you get to the new base. The amount of time is based on whether government housing is available immediately and how hard it is to find a rental in the local area. It's usually 10 to 30 days, but could be as high as 60 days. The housing office can grant TA extensions on a case-by-case basis.

Calculating TLA is very complicated, so it's best to contact the finance office when you get there and have them do it for you.

Overseas Housing Allowance (OHA)

You get an Overseas Housing Allowance (OHA) instead of BAH when you're overseas. This actually covers more than just your rent.

The first part is your *Move-In Housing Allowance (MIHA)*. This is a one-time payment to help make off-base housing habitable. You may find that homes in other countries are quite different from what you're used to (in terms of heating source, appliance size, lack of built-in closets, etc.).

The next part is the actual housing allowance (called the Rental Ceiling). This is the maximum allowance at that location for your spouse's rank and dependent status. It's use-or-lose, so you are only reimbursed for what you actually use. So if the Rental Ceiling is $2,500 and you use $1,700, you don't get to keep the remaining $800. You will only get a payment for $1,700.

def•i•ni•tion

Move-In Housing Allowance (MIHA) is a one-time allowance and is a fixed rate based on the location, not on the military member's rank. It is there to help offset some of the nonrent costs of moving in.

The third part is a perk for overseas families. It's your Utility/Recurring Maintenance Allowance. This isn't designed to pay for all of your utility bills, but it certainly helps out. The amount is fixed based on the location, not on your spouse's rank. So everyone at a specific base gets the same amount.

These allowances are not broken down on your spouse's LES into what is for rent, what is utilities, etc. It's all lumped together under one payment marked OHA. If you want to see the break down, or are curious about the OHA amounts at a base you will be transferring to, you can look it up by location and pay period at http://perdiem.hqda.pentagon.mil/perdiem/ohaform.html.

Overseas Cost of Living Allowance (O-COLA)

There are three factors that can make a huge impact on the amount of O-COLA you get: the exchange rate to local currency, relative cost of items on the economy, and the on-base shopping facilities.

If you live in a country where the exchange rate heavily favors the dollar, and items are also quite cheap off-base, you may not get any O-COLA at all. If, however, you live in a country where the local currency is strong against the dollar, and the prices are quite high on the economy, you will likely get more O-COLA.

Ask the Chief _____

If you have a large Exchange and Commissary at your base, you are expected to do the majority of your shopping there. Because of this, your O-COLA will be much lower than if you did not have these facilities available. This is true even if the local currency is much stronger than the dollar, simply because you don't have to buy as many items on the economy.

The actual O-COLA amount is based on a number of factors including your spouse's rank, time in service, and number of dependents. It is a bimonthly amount and is adjusted frequently. The average amount is $300, but you can look up the rates at http://perdiem.hqda.pentagon.mil/perdiem/ocform.html.

Programs Exclusively for Overseas Military

Some people think living overseas is harder than living in the States. It's certainly different, and can be more challenging to do "normal" things, such as enroll in college. For this reason, there are many programs exclusively for overseas spouses. But be aware, almost all of them require command sponsorship.

What Is Command Sponsorship?

Command sponsorship means you are added onto your spouse's orders for that overseas tour.

When your spouse gets overseas orders for a location that allows spouses, you should be able to get command sponsorship to go with him. Your spouse may have to extend his time in service if the amount of time he has remaining is lower than the minimum accompanied overseas tour for that location.

If you are not command-sponsored, you will get very few military benefits. Command sponsorship is required to ...

◆ Have a concession vehicle.

◆ Get the "with dependents" rates for OHA and O-COLA.

◆ Get the military to pay for you to be moved to the overseas location and back again.

◆ Obtain a ration card for on-base gas and alcohol purchases (if applicable to your base).

◆ Become eligible for overseas spouse education programs.

◆ Enroll in the TRICARE Overseas Prime or TRICARE Global Remote Overseas plans.

◆ Enroll in the TRICARE Dental Program Overseas.

Basically, if you do not have command sponsorship, you have the same benefits as someone visiting that base, not someone stationed there. For example, when I visit my family in England, I can get onto our local U.S. Air Force base, I can buy items at the Commissary and Exchange, and I can use the U.S. Postal Service to ship items back to the states. But I cannot buy gas or alcohol (because they're rationed), or participate in any programs (or receive benefits) restricted to overseas spouses.

You will also be responsible for arranging your own visa and immigration to stay in the country, as it is not linked to your spouse's orders if you're not command-sponsored.

If you are a local national (i.e. you were born in the country your spouse is currently stationed in) you can still become command-sponsored. You'll have to go through the medical and background checks required by U.S. immigration, But, once all of this is done you can become command-sponsored.

Fire in the Hole!

Command sponsorship is a privilege not a right. It can be revoked if you do something detrimental to the command that sponsored you, or to the image of the military. Losing command sponsorship could force you to move back to the United States while your spouse remains to finish out his tour.

Most of this has to be done before you are married, so have your fiancé contact his command and/or the Family Support Center to find out exactly what you need to do. Marriages between locals and U.S. servicemembers are quite common, so they'll probably have a checklist and other resources for you.

Using the GI Bill for Spouses

There are many rumors about using the GI Bill for spouses if you're stationed overseas. I'm afraid these rumors are false. I heard this rumor while stationed overseas but never did anything about it, so either it's changed now, or it was just an urban myth about military benefits.

This should not be confused with the Army program that enables some soldiers reenlisting in critical jobs to transfer up to 50 percent of their GI Bill to their spouse. That is a very real program, and does not require you to be stationed overseas.

Overseas Spouse Education Programs

You may not be able to use his GI Bill, but there are many education grants and tuition-assistance programs that are specifically for command-sponsored spouses living overseas.

The Air Force Aid Society (AFAS) offers the General George S. Brown Spouse Tuition Assistance Program (STAP) to spouses of Air Force personnel who accompany their spouse on an overseas tour. It pays 50 percent of the tuition fee (after other scholarships have been deducted) up to a maximum of $1,500 a year. There is a maximum per term, too, so you can't use it all up in one term. For more information, contact your local AFAS office or go to www.afas.org/Education/body_stapelig.cfm.

The Army Emergency Relief (AER) has a similar program called Overseas Spouse Education Assistance Program (OSEAP). OSEAP is only for the first undergraduate degree. It cannot be used for Master's degree programs. You can also use it for CLEP and DANTES tests, as well as GED preparation and testing.

The maximum is $2,700 per year, but there is a per term maximum too. You do not have to be full time for this program, but you must be attending an on-base education institution. For more information, go to www.aerhq.org/AER_Spouse_Overseas/Downloads/ 07-08%20OSEAP%20description.pdf.

The Navy Marine Corps Relief Society (NMCRS) program is called the Spouse Tuition Aid Program (STAP). This is available for undergraduate or postgraduate studies, and the student is not required to attend full time. As with the other programs, STAP offers a grant of up to 50 percent of the tuition fee that would otherwise come out of your pocket. For undergraduates the maximum is $1,750 per academic year, for graduates it is $2,000. The education establishment must be on-base. For more information go to http://nmcrs.org/education.html.

Space-Available Travel

New regulations as of December 2007 allow dependents to travel more freely without their sponsor. If your spouse has deployment orders for 120 days or more, you can fly anywhere (overseas or within the United States) without your spouse while he is gone.

If you are stationed overseas and your spouse is not deployed, you can fly to most places OCONUS or CONUS unaccompanied, provided you are command-sponsored (and have a letter from the command showing that).

If your spouse is stationed overseas and you are not command-sponsored, you can fly unaccompanied from the United States to his overseas location using space-available travel.

There is a great website about space-available travel at www.spacea.net. It's not an official DoD website, but the information (at least at the time of this writing) is accurate, and they do update it quickly after a regulation change.

Dental Services

We talked about the TRICARE Dental Program in Chapter 3. However, if you live overseas, you don't actually have to be enrolled to receive dental services. You are eligible for "space-available" care at the on-base dental clinic free of charge. Yes, you heard me right, I did just say free—no premiums or co-pays.

Now, this is reliant upon there being a big-enough dental facility for you to get an appointment when you need one. You won't have an assigned dentist, so you'll see whoever is available. But, it's free, so most people don't mind that.

You can continue to keep your dental coverage if you wish. You should get priority for on-base appointments if you do, plus, United Concordia (the TRICARE Dental Program provider) is working with off-base dentists in the vicinity of overseas bases so that you do not have to pay up front and then file the claim paperwork for the reimbursement. This makes it easier and cheaper, and may be the right option for you if it's difficult to get an appointment at your on-base dental clinic. (Co-pays will apply for off-base dental care).

You can find a local dentist who works with United Concordia by going to www.tricaredentalprogram.com and clicking Find An Overseas Host Nation Provider. The direct link is www.tricaredentalprogram.com/tdptws/enrollees/hnp/hnp_search.jsp.

You must be command-sponsored to keep TRICARE dental coverage after you move overseas. If not, you can still use the on-base space-available services free of charge, but if you go off-base, you pay the full cost and will not receive any reimbursement.

Health-Care Services

I talked about TRICARE plans in Chapter 1. The plans overseas are very similar to the CONUS ones regarding who is eligible. So rather than repeating it, the following list shows the name of the overseas plan and which CONUS plan it corresponds to, so you can go back and read it in Chapter 1.

- TRICARE Prime Overseas (equivalent to TRICARE Prime)

- TRICARE Global Overseas Remote (equivalent to TRICARE Remote)

- TRICARE Standard Overseas (equivalent to TRICARE Standard)

- TRICARE Reserve Select Overseas (equivalent to TRICARE Reserve Select)

As with the dental services, you don't have to be enrolled in TRICARE Prime Overseas or TRICARE Global Overseas Remote to receive care. TRICARE Standard is a fee-for-service plan with no premium to pay. The same is true overseas, except that if you get an appointment on-base, you do not pay anything.

The biggest difference is that Prime and Remote enrollees get appointment priority, and they get a Primary Care Manager assigned. Standard enrollees do not. If you're not command-sponsored, you have to stick with TRICARE Standard Overseas.

There are various overseas TRICARE regions, just as there are in the United States. This table shows each region, where it covers, and how to contact them by phone and website. This is also available in Appendix B for quick reference.

There is also a toll-free number for all OCONUS TRICARE Area offices: 1-888-777-8343.

To see all of the plan details and compare overseas plans, go to www. tricare.mil/mybenefit/home/overview/ComparePlans? (note that the ? is part of the link).

Remember to only select the overseas options!

Overseas TRICARE Regions and Contact Information

TRICARE Region	Locations Covered	Phone Number	Website
Europe	Europe, Africa, Middle East	011-49-6302-67-7432	www.tricare.mil/europe
Pacific	Guam, Japan, Korea, Asia, New Zealand, India, Western Pacific remote countries	011-81-6117-43-2036	www.tricare.mil/pacific
Latin America & Canada	Central & South America, the Caribbean Basin, Canada, Puerto Rico, the Virgin Islands	1-706-787-2424	www.tricare.mil/tlac

Footnote: All phone numbers are as if called from the U.S. Replace the 011 with your international dial code if you are outside the U.S.

DoD School vs. Local Community School

You have the choice of using a DoD school on-base (assuming one is available) or putting your child into a local school. Obviously, if you're moving to a country with a different language, you'll probably want to stick with the DoD school, at least until your child has assimilated the language (which children usually do much more quickly than adults).

Even if you speak the same language, it might not be in your child's best interests to go to a local school. Age is a huge factor in this decision. The education requirements for local schools are determined by the country you are living in. So, you will need to do some serious research to determine if it's at the same level that your child would receive in the United States. Sometimes, having attended a local school will put your child at an advantage when she returns to the United States, while other times it will be a disadvantage.

Most accompanied overseas tours are three years. This could cause problems for a child who is in, or approaching, high school, because very often the courses do not translate across to the United States. Advice I've heard from an experienced Family Support Center advisor was not to put a child over the age of 13 or 14 into a non-DoD school. At this age, they are really beginning to work toward high-school graduation. It's much easier to transfer credits from a U.S. DoD school than from a school in another country with a completely different education system.

Language Barriers

There are going to be language barriers whatever country you move to. Even if you go to another English-speaking country, you'll find different words, phraseology, accents, etc. It can be quite unnerving to begin with. George Bernard Shaw once said that America and England are "two nations divided by a common language." I know from personal experience that this is very true. So be prepared for an adjustment period wherever you go.

If you're moving to a country with a completely different language, take a "general usage" class before you go. This will help you with the basics so you can get by when shopping, etc.

The Family Support Center has programs to help you acclimatize to the local culture. These often include language courses.

Minimizing the Stress on the Kids

Moving is hard enough on kids. Moving overseas can be really tough. There are things you can do to make the move smoother and less traumatic for your kids. Most of these are premove, so the earlier you start them, the easier the move will be.

You should be able to find photographs of the location you're moving to by searching online. Seeing photos can take a lot of the fear of the unknown out of the move. It's not as good as visiting in person, but few families can afford that.

Try to find photos of things that will interest your child. Your spouse's sponsor at the new command may be able to help here.

Plan Things to Do in Advance

Almost every base has its own website. While you can find this information from www.militaryhomefront.dod.mil, it's quite complicated to find the official website for each base. A better option is www.military.com's Installation Guide 2.0. The information you'll get on the page is pretty much the same, but there is a prominent "Official Installation Link," which will take you right to the base's website.

Go to www.military.com, and then select Installation Guide from the Community tab. Enter your base's name, or browse by location or branch, etc. to get to the correct listing page. The Official Installation Link is on the top right.

From the official website you'll find links to community services, a welcome guide, etc. In fact, you should have received a welcome packet soon after getting your orders.

Use this information to plan some fun events with your kids. That way they have something to look forward to. It might be a trip to a zoo, or snowboarding in the local mountains, or a beach party. It depends on the location and your child's interests. If you can find activities that are not available at your current location, it can help them have something to look forward to that they can't do until you move.

Resources for Kids

Your Family Support Center has various booklets for kids preparing for a CONUS or OCONUS move. One I particularly like is called *Is There Life After Moving?*, which has stories from other kids about how they felt and how they dealt with the move.

There's another good PDF brochure you can view at www.cfs.purdue.edu/mfri/pages/moving_website/kids_brochure.pdf.

The Military Teens On the Move (MTOM) website at www.defenselink.mil/mtom is another useful resource (this is aimed directly at teenagers to go to the site) The MTOM Kids site (for younger kids) can be accessed from the same link.

Moving Pets

Depending on the country you move to, you may have to quarantine your pets. This can be an expensive and difficult time for all involved. Some countries (such as the U.K.) now offer a no-quarantine option for specific animals, so long as you follow very strict procedures.

Have your spouse check with his sponsor (or call the Family Support Center at the overseas base) as soon as you have orders, to find out what the regulations are for that country.

Often it is still a six-month process, but you get to keep the animal at home rather than having him in a quarantine facility for that time. Because you often don't get written orders until six months in advance, you will need to get organized very quickly so you don't have to go through the quarantine process.

Sometimes families realize that they have to rehouse a pet because their animal is not allowed to be imported (often the case for "dangerous" breeds), because of the health of the pet, or simply the cost of quarantine.

If the country requires six months' quarantine, and it costs $20 per day, it would cost you $3,600 per pet, plus any other fees. That's not to mention the distress the pet would feel being separated from you and not being in a "home" environment. As hard as it is for your family, it's sometimes in the pet's best interest to be rehoused.

If you do decide that you have to rehouse a pet, you should do it sooner rather than later, especially if you have kids. Waiting until the last few days or weeks to find a new home for Fluffy is only going to make the move harder on your children. They will directly associate the move with them losing their beloved pet. If you can plan for Fluffy to be with a new family a few months before you move (well before you start packing and doing other moving-related tasks) it will become less of an issue for your child when you do actually move.

The Least You Need to Know

◆ You must be command-sponsored to get most of the overseas family benefits.

◆ You do not need to be enrolled in TRICARE Prime or the TRICARE Dental Program to receive free "space-available" care on-base.

◆ DoD schools are usually a better option for kids in high school, particularly nearing graduation.

◆ Photographs of the new location will help ease the fear of the unknown for your child.

◆ Some countries have a no-quarantine option for transporting pets, but the regulations are very strict, so make sure you follow them to the letter.

Part 3

Help, My Spouse Is Getting Deployed

As more and more of our military are deployed overseas, this part is critical to helping you and your family survive at home. Here I cover pre-deployment planning, how to deal with the actual deployment and common crises that happen, post-deployment, and also what happens if your spouse is injured in the field, or worse. I also cover how to plan for your spouse's retirement and how your military benefits will change.

DON'T BOTHER DADDY. HE'S BEEN DEPLOYED TO THE KITCHEN TO DO THE DISHES...

BARR

Chapter 11

Pre-Deployment Planning

In This Chapter

- ◆ Pre-deployment legal paperwork
- ◆ Life insurance for both of you
- ◆ When you'll need a Power of Attorney
- ◆ Planning for emergencies while he's gone
- ◆ Preparing the kids

It doesn't matter where they're going or for how long, deployment is never much fun. Deployments can be scheduled months in advance, or you could have only a few days' notice. In a time of war (as we are at the time of writing) that's just the way it goes. Pretending that it won't ever happen to you is foolish.

Planning for the "what if" scenario will make it much easier if your spouse does get picked to go at the last minute. Having all of the paperwork done means more time for him to spend with you and the kids. If that's not an incentive, I don't know what is!

The Difference Between a Deployment and IA

Most people who go deployed to the Middle East at the moment are going in units, squadrons, crews, etc. However, the Navy has an additional program that sends individuals out to fill specific job needs. They call it Individual Augmentation, or IA.

IA is usually a 12-month tour. It is always unaccompanied, so you will not be following him. Neither will you be able to visit him there. However, he may get a couple of weeks R&R during the deployment in which he may be able to visit you (we'll talk about that more in Chapter 12).

Going on an IA is good for evaluations and promotion. IA assignments are usually boots on the ground, but not all are in Iraq, Afghanistan, etc. So the danger level really varies a lot.

The program is being changed at the moment (2008). Previously, when individuals volunteered (or were "voluntold") they left their current duty (usually a shore billet) to go IA, then returned to their previous command. They tried to give the sailor a few months or a few days notice. This made it very hard on sailors and families at shore commands. At one of our shore duties, almost a third of our command was IA.

Now, the selection process is being integrated into standard sea/shore rotations. So your spouse could pick an IA billet just like a one-year unaccompanied tour when he comes up for orders. He would go IA after he finishes his current tour. He would also get orders for the following duty station (after his IA is over) so you (his family) can relocate prior to the IA if you want to.

This is making it much easier for families to plan, and taking a lot of the stress and anxiety out of the program. For more information go to www.nffsp.org and click Individual Augmentees on the left bar. You can download the IA Family Handbook here.

The Legal Stuff

There are various legal documents you need to have taken care of before your spouse goes deployed.

Creating a Will

You can pick up will worksheets from your legal office. This goes through everything you need to think about when creating a will. Once it's completed, you will meet with the attorney at the legal office who will actually write up the will for you. You'll actually have two appointments, one to discuss the will worksheet after you've completed it, and the other to actually sign the drawn up document.

It's smart to create both of your wills at the same time. If nothing else, it opens a dialogue about these things. Death is not something anyone wants to think about, particularly pre-deployment, but it's very important for both of you no matter what age you are.

Be aware, it can take a week or more to get an appointment, and wills take time to write so don't wait until the last minute.

Power of Attorney

There are many times that you will need a Power of Attorney (POA) while he's gone. A "General" POA technically gives you power to make any legal decisions on behalf of your spouse. But many places don't accept them. You will need a "Special" POA to accept a place in base housing or in military childcare, to renew your ID card, to buy or sell a vehicle/property, to access financial accounts, resolve pay issues, etc.

Have the legal office draw up a Special POA for any of these eventualities that might occur for you while he is gone. They can put it all in one document which makes it easier for you. A POA generally lasts for one year, so if your spouse is gone for longer make sure the legal office knows that.

Life Insurance (SGLI)

The military offers a life insurance plan called SGLI (Servicemember's Group Life Insurance) which is very reasonable in cost (currently 7 cents per $1,000 of coverage, plus $1 for the TSGLI rider, which I'll explain in a moment). The minimum coverage is $50,000 and it goes up in $50,000 increments, up to $400,000. It can be deducted from your spouse's paycheck pretax. The current premium amounts went into effect July 1, 2006 and are still accurate as of March 2008.

SGLI Coverage and Premium Amounts

Coverage	Monthly Premium
$50,000	$4.50
$100,000	$8.00
$150,000	$11.50
$200,000	$15.00
$250,000	$18.50
$300,000	$22.00
$350,000	$25.50
$400,000	$29.00

Traumatic Injury Protection Rider

Included in the SGLI premium in the above table is a $1 premium for TSGLI. This is the Traumatic Injury Protection rider for SGLI. It's $1 no matter which level of coverage you choose. You cannot buy SGLI without the additional $1 TSGLI rider (which is why I included it in the monthly premium in the table).

TSGLI coverage pays your spouse a lump-sum amount for a traumatic injury. The amount ranges from $25,000 to $100,000. You can see what is paid for each injury at www.insurance.va.gov/sgliSite/popups/ ScheduleOfLosses.htm.

SGLI and TSGLI are available to active-duty, ready reserve, National Guard, midshipmen of the four service academies, and members of the Reserve Officer Training Corps.

For more information about SGLI and TSGLI go to www.insurance. va.gov/sgliSite/SGLI/SGLI.htm.

Family Life Insurance

SGLI for military families is called FSGLI. The premium is based on the dependent's age and the amount of coverage desired. The minimum coverage is $10,000, and maximum is $100,000. It's very inexpensive; for example, if you're under 35, the $10,000 rate is 55 cents per month.

If you choose to max out at $100,000, you still only pay $5.50. You can see the rates for each age at www.insurance.va.gov/sgliSite/FSGLI/fsgliPremiums.htm.

Other Important Considerations

Make sure you have all passwords for your computers, e-mail accounts, and any online bill payment sites you use.

Most people rely on internet to communicate with their deployed spouse, so have everything at hand that you'd require to completely reformat the drive and reinstall the operating system and all software, if it gets a unresolvable virus or crashes.

Taxes

Make sure you're up to date on your tax filing. If your spouse is deployed during tax season, he is eligible for an extension. The amount is the entire length of deployment in the Combat Zone plus 180 days.

There are many tax programs and benefits for military families. Go to www.irs.gov/individuals/military/index.html for details.

If you wish to file your joint taxes before your spouse returns, you can do it (a good idea if you're expecting a large refund). I suggest you get your base *VITA* office to help you, unless you know all the deductions that are available to military families.

def•i•ni•tion

VITA stands for Volunteer Income Tax Assistance, and most bases have an office open during tax season. It is completely free.

Bank Accounts and Finances

Even if your spouse always deals with the financial aspect of your lives, it's important for you to know what's going on. You are responsible for managing it while he is gone.

You need to know and have access to all financial accounts you or your spouse have. This can be a touchy subject, because if you've always had separate accounts, he might not want to relinquish that. However, if he pays all of the bills, you're going to need to have access to the account. Plus, you'll need to know what bills to expect and when.

I've found a "deployment account" specifically for my husband when he's deployed to be very useful. I keep it funded so my husband can withdraw cash without worrying about any bills that might be going out.

You must have access to whatever account receives his paycheck. Often they don't have access to computers and therefore to their LES. You should ask your spouse to set up a Restricted Access Pin for My Pay so you can access his LES, too.

If his pay is not right, you need to identify it as soon as possible. The worst scenarios are either that they grossly underpaid you and you can't meet your monthly financial obligations, or (even worse) they overpaid you.

If your spouse is gone for eight months and is overpaid $150 per month, you might not notice it (particularly if his pay became tax-free or he's eligible for other allowances). But, when the finance office changes his pay again after the deployment, they will more than likely catch their mistake. Now you've got to pay back $1,200 that you have probably already spent.

Having access to the account and LES could mean you catch this error quickly. Then the finance office can fix it (or at least you know to set the money aside to be paid back later).

We'll talk more about the pay, allowances, and benefits you get when your spouse is deployed in Chapter 12.

Emergency Planning

Things always go wrong when your spouse is deployed—that's just the way it is. So you need to plan for it, and know what you'll do if it does happen.

If your location is prone to natural disasters (hurricanes, flood, wild-fires, etc.) make sure you have an emergency kit on hand. You will want a wind-up radio and flashlight (i.e. no batteries needed). You'll also want enough nonperishable food and water to last you a week, and any medicines your family needs. Contact your local American Red Cross to get a list of other items they suggest for an emergency kit in your area.

You also need a plan of action for what you will do in the event of an emergency. Where will you go? Who will you stay with? What will you do with pets? What items will you evacuate with?

Red Cross Training

If you have a child at home, I suggest you attend American Red Cross CPR training. Your spouse already has it, but it's always a good idea to have at least one adult in the house knowing CPR. I hope you never need to use it, but you'd be devastated if you ever did need it and didn't know how to do it properly.

Helping Kids Prepare for the Deployment

Kids react to deployments differently. They may become clingier, or emotionally detached, or they may thrive on the challenge and become more independent, craving more responsibility. Or they may become introverted and not want to be around other people. Young children may regress (potty training, language skills, etc.), and grades and behavior at school may slip a bit.

On the run up to a deployment, there are many things you can do to make the transition easier for your children. The more work you put in here, the easier the actual deployment will be for your kids (and consequently for you, too!)

- ◆ Talk to your children about the upcoming deployment and where Dad will be. It may be helpful to use a world map to give them an idea of where he is in relation to home.

- ◆ Give kids as much notice about the deployment as you can. That way they can have time to get used to the idea.

- ◆ Get the kids involved in the decisions about routine changes and explain why they are necessary. Give them choices (either of which work for you) so they can make the decision rather than having a change imposed on them.

◆ Talk about the family rules and reinforce that they won't be changing when Dad is gone, even though some of the routines will change. They will push boundaries when Dad leaves, but you must remain consistent.

◆ Try to change routines (such as a longer day at daycare, being picked up from an activity by a friend's parent, etc.) before your spouse deploys. That way any logistic problems can be solved in advance, and your child can get used to the change before Dad leaves.

◆ Answer questions honestly and in a matter-of-fact way. Reinforce the positives.

◆ Young kids may think Dad is leaving because they did something wrong or that Dad doesn't love them anymore. It's very important for you and your spouse to reiterate that this is not the case. Do this as much by action as by words. Make sure each child has "special time" with Dad shortly before he leaves. It might be going out for ice cream, or going to play at the park, but whatever it is, make sure it's a positive experience for the child and that the child is the center of attention.

◆ Tell your child's schoolteacher or daycare provider that his Dad's deploying, and keep them informed about discussions and concerns that have arisen at home. Make sure you do this well in advance, because pre-deployment anxiety can be as bad for kids as during the actual deployment (think about how you feel on the run up to a deployment—your kids are having just as hard a time, but they can't rationalize as well as you can).

◆ Make something with your children that can be hidden in Dad's luggage. Pictures, collages of photos, etc. are good ideas because they won't crush in transit, and can be stuck up on the wall next to your spouse's bed.

◆ Create a deployment paper chain. You can choose whether to have one link per day, week, or month. Your choice will largely depend on where you will hang it up and how long your spouse is gone. Always overestimate (your kids will be excited to rip off more than one per day, but if you have to add more links on, they'll be disappointed).

- Paste a picture of the child with Dad doing an activity they enjoy on a jar. Each day that Dad is gone, give your child a nickel or dime to put in the jar. When Dad returns they can use the money they've saved to do something special with Dad.

- Make a photo calendar for each child with photos of them with Dad doing something in each month of the year. You can do a "family" one too.

- Say a proper goodbye as a family so the kids know that the changes you've talked about with them will be coming into effect now.

- Get a copy of the Talk, Listen, Connect DVD through your Family Support Center or www.militaryonesource.com. It features Elmo from Sesame Street and has some really good tips for young children dealing with deployment.

Daddy Dolls, Inc.

In my opinion, Daddy Dolls (www.hugahero.com) are a must for all kids with a deployed parent. A Daddy Doll (officially called a Hug-A-Hero doll) is a plush doll with a photograph of Dad printed on it. You upload a full-length photo to their site and select the size and backing fabric; then they cut out the background around the figure and do a high-quality transfer onto white fabric (as you can see in the following photo).

They are super-soft and also washable (very useful for long deployments, or if your spouse deploys frequently).

My two-year-old daughter's Daddy Doll arrived a couple of weeks after my husband deployed. The excitement on her face was just priceless. It made all the difference for her. Instead of asking for Daddy, looking for him around the house, and looking out the window waiting for him to come back from work, she was happy to share her daily activities with her Daddy Doll. He sat at the Christmas table with us, he went shopping with us, and she slept curled up with her arm over him every night. It's made the time apart much easier for her, even at such a young age.

The two founders of Daddy Dolls, Inc. and their children with their Daddy Dolls.

It was wonderful for my husband, too, because he could see her interacting with it, and obviously very happy hugging and playing with it. She treats it like a photograph of her Dad that she can hug and play with. My husband said it was like he was able to be there for the different events he missed.

One thing I love about Daddy Dolls, Inc., is that the owners are two Marine Corps wives, and the people who make the dolls are all military families.

As well as dolls, they also make photo dog tags and photo pillows for kids who are too old for dolls. It doesn't have to be Dad either. Many military families are displaced from extended family, and "Grandma" dolls are very popular!

It takes about 3-4 weeks to receive your doll, so order it early. However, if it arrives after Dad leaves (as my daughter's did) it will still be a wonderful surprise.

DreamCap

Stress can often manifest itself as nightmares or restless sleep. If your child has problems with this, you might find a DreamCap helps her. The DreamCap works on the power of belief. If the child "believes" that the fabric cap she wears at night will block her nightmares, then it will.

The owner of the company, Jim Ramey, is a retired Navy Chief Petty Officer. He currently has a buy-one-get-one-free offer for military families, so if you have multiple kids, or a friend who wants one, this is a good way to get two of them. Go to www.stopbaddreams.com for more information or to order.

Plan Ahead for Special Events (Birthdays, Christmas, etc.)

There is almost always some special event occurring while your spouse is gone. If you can plan ahead for this, you can still make it a special day. Here are a few things your spouse can do before he leaves or while he's gone:

- ◆ Write birthday/Christmas cards.
- ◆ Make a video greeting to be played on the special occasion.
- ◆ See if his deployment site and your base have video call capabilities. If so, this could be a great way for your spouse to talk to his family on the special day.
- ◆ Consider having an "official" birthday or Christmas celebration once Dad is home (if it's pretty close). You can do both celebrations. Kids love that!

Most commands have a pre-deployment brief before the deployment. Be proactive and ask your spouse when it is. They have a lot on their minds and you don't want to miss it. This is the place to ask any questions you might have, and also to get information about command support while your spouse is gone.

This meeting is a good time to meet other families in the same situation. The best support you will get while your spouse is gone is from other people in the same situation.

In the next chapter I will talk about The Deployment Cycle. This will affect you even a month before your spouse deploys, so make sure to read about this.

The Least You Need To Know

- You will need a Special Power of Attorney to do many things on behalf of your spouse while he's deployed.

- Life insurance coverage for you and your spouse is available through the SGLI and FSGLI programs.

- Deployed servicemembers can get a tax filing extension.

- Talk to your kids about changes and try to implement major routine adjustments before your spouse deploys.

- Get a Daddy Doll and make other deployment aids for your kids before Dad deploys.

- Make sure to attend the pre-deployment brief.

Chapter 12

During the Deployment

In This Chapter

- ◆ The good side of deployments (extra pay)
- ◆ Saving during deployments
- ◆ The emotional roller coaster
- ◆ Keep the communication
- ◆ Supporting kids through deployments
- ◆ Making R&R an enjoyable experience for everyone

We've talked about the planning side of deployments, but what about the actual deployment itself? This is one of the most challenging times for most families, but knowing what to expect and how to make the best of it will make the deployment far easier for you.

Pay and Benefits

Let's start with the good news. While your spouse is gone you're going to make a lot more money, particularly if he's in a hazard duty zone.

Family Separation Allowance (FSA)

I've mentioned this before. FSA (also called Family Sep.) is the $250 monthly allowance you get when your spouse is gone. FSA is authorized for servicemembers deployed for over 30 days.

Hostile Fire Pay (HFP)/Imminent Danger Pay (IDP)

HFP/IDP is only for servicemembers in a designated hazard duty zone. The amount is $225 per month for all pay grades. The good news is that they only have to be in that zone for one day of the month to get the allowance for the entire month. So if they arrive on April 29 and then depart on September 2, they get HFP/IDP for six months even though they're actually only there for four months plus three days.

Hardship Duty Pay—Location (HDP-L)

Depending on the location, your spouse may be entitled to a hardship duty pay. It varies from $50 to $150 (based on the location, not your spouse's rank). The charts are available at www.defenselink.mil/comptroller/fmr/07a/07a_17.pdf (starts on page 33). Iraq, Afghanistan, and Kuwait are all $100 per month.

Hazardous Duty Incentive Pay (HDIP)

This is most commonly called Flight Pay, but it covers far more than just flight hazards (such as parachuting, working with demolition, and working on the flight deck of a ship).

For crew members (those who actually fly) the amount varies by rank (from $150–$250). Parachutists' ("jump") pay, and HDIP for people who don't actually fly, is $150 per month for all pay grades. Parachutists who do HALO jumps (High Altitude Low Opening) may be eligible for a higher rate (currently $225).

Your spouse may be eligible for this pay when he's not deployed (such as crew member flight pay), or it may be an additional pay that he receives only when deployed.

Per Diem

Assuming your spouse is living in military housing (could be a tent, trailer, or actual barracks if he's lucky) he is authorized $3.50 per day for Per Diem. If he is off-base at a hotel, the amount can be determined using the Per Diem calculator at http://perdiem.hqda.pentagon.mil/perdiem/perdiemrates.html.

How Much Extra per Month

Let's have a look at how this all totals up:

$250	Family Separation
$150	Hazard Duty Incentive Pay
$100	Hardship Duty Pay—Location (Iraq/Afghanistan)
$225	Hostile Fire/Imminent Danger Pay
$725	**Total per Month**

Assuming your spouse is eligible for all of these pays you will be receiving an extra $725 per month.

Don't forget that if he's in a combat zone, it's all tax-free (as is his basic pay). So it's not unrealistic for you to get an extra $900 per month while he's gone. That's a lot of money, $5,400 over a six-month deployment. The question is, what do you do with it? Many people spend it (particularly if it's their first deployment). But there is a much better option.

Savings Deposit Program (SDP)

The Savings Deposit Program is available to servicemembers in designated combat zones who are eligible for Hostile Fire/Imminent Danger Pay. The military member can deposit up to $10,000 over the term of the deployment into this account, which accrues at 10 percent interest.

This is an investment program, so withdrawals are limited while your spouse is in the combat zone. He can make withdrawals for emergencies, but this isn't the place to put money you may need.

He can withdraw the funds after he returns if you wish, or you can leave it in there. Interest stops accruing 90 days after your spouse leaves the combat zone though.

You can read more about this at www.dfas.mil/army2/investmentoptions/savingsdepositprogramsdp.html. It is available to all active-duty and reservists in the designated regions. They can begin making deposits on the thirty-first day of being in the combat zone.

The Deployment Cycle

The emotional cycle of deployment is nothing new. It was first explained by Kathleen Vestal Logan in 1987 (in a *Proceedings* magazine). There are seven stages which occur throughout three phases of deployment (pre-deployment, deployment, and reintegration).

The Emotional Cycle of Deployment

Stage	Name	Emotions/Common Actions	When it Occurs
1	Anticipation of Loss	Arguing, anxiety, sadness, resentment	Pre-deployment
2	Detachment and Withdrawal	Emotional withdrawal, numbness	Last days before deployment
3	Emotional Disorgani-zation	Guilt, depressed, lonely, overwhelmed, indecisive	First six weeks of deployment
4	Recovery and Stabilization	Able to copy, new routine in place, more confidence, sometimes loneliness and feeling of isolation	From end of third stage until four to six weeks before end of deployment
5	Anticipation of Homecoming	Apprehension of changes you've made/not made, excited, nervous, happy	Last few weeks before end of deployment

Stage	Name	Emotions/Common Actions	When it Occurs
6	Renegotiation	Brief honeymoon period, may feel loss of independence/freedom, learning how to work as a couple again, increased frustration	Homecoming until up to six weeks later
7	Reintegration and Stabilization	Relaxed, comfortable, back in routine	Four to six weeks post-deployment

The deployment cycle is an emotional cycle that you, your spouse, and kids will go through while he's gone. It begins before he leaves, usually with arguments. Emotionally it's easier to be separated from someone if you are mad at them. Pre-deployment becomes a lot less stressful once you know how to identify that you're both doing this and deal with it better.

The first month of the deployment is usually the worst for emotional instability. This is when most of the day-to-day changes happen to your routine. You may feel lonely, abandoned, lost, angry, upset at him, upset at the military, feel like you can't cope with all the responsibility on your own, guilty for having fun with the kids or your friends while he's gone, etc. It's all completely normal. Your emotions are going to go haywire for a few weeks. But, again, knowing that this is normal can help you deal with it more productively.

Remember, all the changes that are affecting you are doing the same to your children, only they can't rationalize them. So you will likely see them pushing boundaries, acting up, etc. Of course, this is just at the time when you could really use them being little angels. The important thing is not to overreact. Don't let them get away with things because Dad's gone, and equally, don't overreact because you're already very stressed.

I suggest you get involved with your unit/command Family Readiness Group (FRG) where everyone's in the same situation, so you can support each other. If you don't have an active FRG, then look to some of the online forums for military spouses. There will be many spouses on there who are dealing with the same issues, frustrations, and feelings as you. There are also many who have dealt with deployments before.

The good news is that everything settles down after the first month or so. You'll get into a routine for how to manage things at home, your communication will be more effective with your spouse, and he'll settle into his job out there.

For the majority of the deployment, this is how it will stay. Although you miss him a lot, you'll realize that you can cope on your own. Then, as homecoming approaches, you'll find the anxiety returns. Usually it's the last month that this starts. You might start getting stressed about getting the house right, how you'll react when he's home, whether your relationship will be the same, and if he'll have changed; you might worry if you've put on or lost weight if he'll still be attracted to you. The kids will be getting excited, too.

Once he gets back, there is an adjustment period, too, but we'll talk more about that in Chapter 13.

Communicating with Your Spouse

During the first few weeks that he's gone, your communication will probably be very erratic. Most of the time he won't talk about feelings, or really anything that's going on. It can be very frustrating for spouses who write long e-mails or letters to get one-sentence responses. But this makes sense in a way.

Much of the time, they are limited on their internet access and may only get 15 minutes a couple of times a week (if that). So if you've e-mailed him every day since he left (and he's had a few days in transit to get there), he's got a lot of reading to catch up on. He may literally only have time to send back a short response. It doesn't mean he's not interested. Usually it just means he's run out of time.

Your role while he's gone is support. If you don't hear from him for a week or so, don't get mad at him when he finally calls. Be very glad that he did call.

Often they don't get a lot of chances to phone home. Plus, they need decompressing time after coming back from a mission. This may be watching DVDs or playing video games. It's not that they see these things as more important than you, but they may be too stressed or tired to call home, and may need to zone out. It may have been an emotionally stressful mission for them and they're not able to bring emotions back yet. It's better for them to wait and use their phone call allowance when they are in a better mood and more able to talk to you.

Roles tend to reverse during deployments. He may have always been there to support you, but while he's deployed your main role is to support him. Don't expect to vent about the hard day you've had. You probably can't even imagine some of the days he's having, nor can he tell you about most of it.

Usually after the first four to six weeks, your spouse will be better settled, and you'll find you're getting the conversations you want,

Top's Tips

Don't whine about him not contacting you or his lack of emotion when he does. All this will do is make him want to call you less!

Ask the Chief

It can be very frustrating for your spouse to not be allowed to tell you what's going on, or why he's stressed. Most people who have security clearances are used to this, but for those who have always been able to share the ins and outs of daily life, this change can be very hard for all concerned.

and he'll probably be expressing more emotion (telling you he loves you and misses you, etc.) So don't panic if in the first few weeks you don't hear the L word very much. It doesn't mean that he doesn't love you. He's just still getting adjusted.

Letters, E-mails, and Webcams

We must be thankful as spouses that we usually have means of communication other than letters. I've heard wives complain about not hearing from their husband once a week. Before the internet, families often went a month or more with no contact.

The amount of communication, and type, will largely depend on where he is. Some places simply don't have phones. Others have a phone bank where your spouse can use an international calling card to call you. Some locations use DSN lines (official military phone lines) to enable him to call. But be aware, your calls are usually monitored.

You'll hear the word OPSEC quite often from your spouse, his command, and other people. OPSEC stands for Operational Security. There are many things your spouse will not be able to tell you about because of OPSEC.

You must be proactive about this, too. You mustn't talk about specific dates that he will be returning, their travel route, what command he's with, even where he is currently located. It may seem a little paranoid, but if you assume that every e-mail you write and phone call you make is being intercepted by the enemy, then you won't say something that could put someone in danger. It may seem innocuous to you, but OPSEC is cumulative. If they get one piece of information from you, another from someone else, and so on, they can build the big picture.

Sending a Little TLC from Home

Care packages are wonderful. They send a bit of home to our loved ones and show them that we really do care. But, you need to make sure that you do it properly. It's smart to wait until they're out there to find out what they actually need (and get their address). Often they need toiletries, good razor blades, powdered energy drinks, candy (always a favorite), etc. Other times it will be something specific like underarmor shirts, or things they forgot or didn't think they'd need.

> **From Seasoned Spouses**
>
> When my husband deployed, I got a talking photo album. It has a record button for each photo slot for you to leave a 10-second message. This went down really well. I was able to get our 2-year-old daughter to say things on some of them, too. This is so precious because not only can he see his family, but he can also hear them.

Above all, though, photos, letters, and personal touches are the most precious. Yes, they love the "stuff," but it's the nonconsumables that they really treasure.

Don't send anything irreplaceable, such as original photographs if you don't have them on your computer or the negatives somewhere safe, important trinkets, and so on. Assume that he will not be bringing back anything you've sent. Most of the time they will, but sometimes things get lost or damaged.

The USPS has a flat-rate Priority Mail box specifically for APO/FPO shipping. It is 12"×12"×5.5" and has "America Supports You" written on the side. You also get a $2 discount off the retail price, so you only pay $10.95 no matter what the weight of the package. Delivery time is usually 10-14 days.

When Emergencies Occur

If there is an emergency at home (death in the family, critical injury, etc.) you can send an Emergency Red Cross Message to your spouse. The American Red Cross caseworker will verify the information you give him and then ensure that the message is sent. It doesn't matter where your spouse is; they will get the message to him and then follow up with you.

Sometimes the command will bring your spouse home. It depends on the nature of the emergency and how time-critical his return is.

If your spouse is active-duty and you live with him or her in the United States, you can call the American Red Cross to send an emergency message toll-free at 1-877-272-7337.

 Ask the Chief

If a child is born while the father is deployed, the mother can send a birth announcement to the new dad using the American Red Cross message system.

If your spouse is active-duty but you live overseas, contact your on-base Red Cross office, or call the base's main number and tell them you need to send an Emergency Red Cross Message to your deployed spouse, and they'll connect you.

If your spouse is a reservist, National Guard, civilian, or if you do not live in the same house as him, you should contact your local American Red Cross chapter and they'll help you. Go to www.redcross.org/where/where.html to find your local chapter.

You should have been given the name and contact information for your unit/command point of contact at the pre-deployment brief. The Army have FRG Leaders, the Navy have Ombudsmen, the Marine Corps have Key Volunteers, and the Air Force have Key Spouses. Your unit/ command may have another designated person. They are great people to contact when you need help. They work as the link between the command and the families, and they will help you wherever they can.

Communication Survival Tips

Communication is the key. If you can effectively communicate, even if it's only once every week or so, you will find the deployment goes much smoother (and quicker).

Webcams

Webcams are great whether or not your spouse has one available. Most of the time he will be able to view yours, so he can see you and the kids even if you can't see him. This will mean the world to him.

Phone Calls

Phone bills can be astronomical. You can buy calling cards that have decent rates to Iraq, but other countries in the region can be much higher. Even if you have an international calling plan on your home phone, you can be stung with very high rates, so make sure to check the per-minute costs.

From Seasoned Spouses

My international calling plan for my home phone gives me a 2-cents-per-minute rate to England to call my family. I foolishly assumed the rate to where my husband was deployed would be decent, too. Had I checked, I'd have seen that it was almost a dollar a minute. I discovered this when I got my first bill. Ouch.

If you do choose a calling card, make sure to check all the additional fees (disconnect fee, maintenance fee, etc.). Sometimes the one with the lowest per-minute rate is actually not the cheapest for you.

Many people are taking Skype or Vonage phones with them so they can connect with family back home very inexpensively (often free). Other people buy cell phones within the country they're deployed to. These tend to be more expensive. Some people are able to get international service for their regular cell phone.

Daddy's Story Time

If you have young kids who enjoy story time, one thing they will love is your spouse recording himself reading favorite stories.

You can read along with the child with the book in front of you. Have your spouse read it as if the camera is your child. So look right into the camera and pause where he normally would when asking the child a question, or for words the child normally likes to say herself. That makes it far more interactive.

 Ask the Chief _____

If your spouse doesn't take his cell phone, most companies will allow him to temporarily disconnect the service until he returns (there may be a small monthly fee).

Video for Dad

Taking video of the kids is wonderful, too. You can upload to YouTube and set it to private so only you and your spouse can view it. Check that your spouse can access this site from his location before you upload the video clips. Many locations block sites like YouTube, MySpace, Facebook, Flickr, etc.

Even if he can't view it out there, he will be able to catch up on all the fun things the kids have been doing while he's been gone. This is particularly important when you have young children who change dramatically in a matter of a few months. Seeing the progression in the videos will give your spouse something to hang onto. He won't feel like he's missed such a long period of his children's lives.

If he has access to a DVD player you could make a DVD of the video clips and send it in a care package.

Consistency for Kids

Consistency is the key to a happy child, whether both parents are at home or only one. Everything you do must be consistent. You can't let children get away with something one day and then enforce the rule another day. You'll just end up with a confused child who doesn't know the boundaries, and so will constantly push them. This is not good for your stress level! Keeping consistent when your spouse is gone is very important, and will help you and your kids cope far better.

Discipline

When a parent leaves, it's easy to let things slide, and let kids get away with things that are normally against the rules. You may think you're being kinder, but it's actually worse for the kids. The more you stick to the family rules, the better.

Please, never say, "wait until your Dad gets home" as a means of discipline. All this will do is undermine your authority as a disciplinarian, and make your child terrified of seeing his Dad when he does come home. In the meantime, the kids will continue to push your buttons and leave you so stressed you don't know if you're coming or going. Discipline needs to be immediate for the child to link it to the bad behavior (if I throw toys at my brother I have to sit in time out and the toys get taken away).

If you're having a hard time dealing with discipline issues, contact your Family Support Center. If the child is under three, the New Parent Support Team will likely be able to give you some suggestions. Otherwise, the Family Support Center should be able to refer you to someone else who can help. Talk to other families in your FRG, too. They may have some suggestions of things that are working with their kids.

Routines

This is part of consistency. Routines change; that's how it is when you go from two people helping out to one person doing everything. The point is to be as consistent as you can with whatever changes you make to the routine.

If your spouse deploys frequently, set up "deployment routines." This way the kids get to understand that when Dad is home, there is a home routine, and when he's gone, it is the deployment routine. Both should be kept consistent as much as possible. This will help your kids cope with the changes far better.

Things You Can Do to Help Your Kids

As well as the other things I've mentioned, here are a few things you can do that will make the deployment easier for your children:

◆ Have your spouse take a photo of where he sleeps. Having a picture of Dad's bed with pictures of his family stuck on the wall, and seeing him smiling in the picture, will give your kids an image to bring to mind when they think about Dad being deployed.

◆ Keep a picture of your child with his dad in his room, and keep photos of the family around the house. This helps keep Dad part of everyday life even when he's gone.

◆ Don't put everything on hold when your spouse leaves. If there are activities you do as a family (bowling night, pizza night, etc.), continue them. Daddy Dolls often end up "playing" board games on family game night.

◆ Plan a special activity for each child while your spouse is gone, so they have something to look forward to.

◆ Limit and monitor TV watching. There are some very disturbing images from the news and movies that could really affect your child. You need to explain to kids that what they see on the news is usually the worst side of it, and may be far away from your spouse's location.

◆ Make sure your kids know they can always talk to you about questions, concerns, something someone's said, etc. Don't brush them off, even if they're asking the same question for the fifteenth time. It may be something that really concerns them and they need the constant reassurance. It's far better that they ask you than to dwell on it and get depressed or stressed out.

◆ If you do see signs of withdrawal, stress, or depression, talk to your child's pediatrician. They should have some suggestions, and will determine if it's a clinical issue.

How to Stay Sane at Home

First, get involved in your Family Readiness Group (FRG) or spouse organization. It doesn't matter if you're single or have kids: everyone needs support at some point. This is precisely what these groups are designed for. These are great networking places too, and male spouses are definitely welcome!

If you don't work, try taking up a hobby, or plan to do things with other people with deployed spouses so you don't get bored.

If you work and have kids, you may feel a little overwhelmed. Okay, more than just a little. Just remember, you are not superhuman, nor does anyone expect you to be. If it helps, make a to-do list of important things, in order of priority. Not folding the laundry for a few days is not the end of the world, but because it's a visual thing, you might be tempted to take care of that when there are actually more important things to do. If you work your way down your list, and don't get time for everything, then at least you did the most important things.

If you're a stay-at-home parent, you might consider a kids-swap with another parent from your command. It could just be for a few hours one afternoon a week, but it's time for *you*. Don't feel guilty about it— everyone needs a break, and while your spouse is gone, you're not going to get that any other way. Family may offer to help out, too. Take help when it is offered!

Making the Most of R&R

Rest and Recuperation (R&R) is not guaranteed, but people who are deployed for 270 days are eligible and most get it. It's basically two weeks of time off. Your spouse can fly back to the United States and see you, or you can join him somewhere closer (such as in Europe) if you'd prefer. The military pays to fly him, but if you choose to meet him somewhere else, your flights and accommodations are your own responsibility.

Honestly, if you have kids the best advice I can give you is to take a vacation. If Dad comes home for just two weeks, it's going to be much harder on the kids to let him go again. If you instead meet him at, say, Disneyland, or some other place away from home and make the R&R

trip a family vacation, it will be much easier to transition your kids back into Dad not being there. If he's not been "home" with you, they won't have tried to assimilate Dad back into their day-to-day life yet. Plus, it's a great memory for the kids (and your spouse).

In my opinion, this is a good use of some of the extra money you've been getting while your spouse is on deployment.

It's important that your spouse stick to the kids' rules you've been enforcing. He may be tempted to not enforce them, to "be the nice guy," but that will only make it harder for you when he's gone again, and also when he's transitioning back into the family after the deployment is over. Make sure you're on the same page from square one. If in doubt, "What did your Mom say?" is a great response to a request. Most kids don't think to lie about what Mom said! You should plan to use this, too. If your husband made a decision (even if you disagree with it), you must be united or the kids will play you off against each other.

For tips about making your R&R a good experience, go to www. militaryonesource.com and search the term "R&R." The top hit will be "What to Expect on an R&R During Times of Deployment." This is a really great article. You can get to it directly at http://tinyurl.com/ 2lsmu8.

The Least You Need to Know

- ◆ You will get more money while your spouse is gone. The Savings Deposit Plan can help you make the most of it.

- ◆ Being very emotional is common during deployments. It's part of the deployment cycle.

- ◆ Sending care packages can be wonderful for your spouse, but make sure you're sending things he can't get there.

- ◆ Keep consistent with your kids regarding boundaries and discipline.

- ◆ Plan things to do throughout the deployment that your children can look forward to.

- ◆ If possible, make R&R a vacation. Your spouse needs it, and you probably do, too!

Chapter 13

Post-Deployment

In This Chapter

- Common fears and expectations for homecoming
- Dealing with routine changes
- The financial implication of the end of deployment
- Reintegrating your spouse into your family

Homecoming is an exciting time. You and your spouse may have been apart a few months or for over a year. Either way you'll be excited, nervous, and probably at least a little stressed. Everyone has "goals" for while their spouse is deployed; it may be weight loss, it might be decorating, or getting projects done. You will almost certainly not meet all of your goals. Don't worry about it. Your spouse is not going to be upset. He's just going to be glad to be home. He might actually like to get involved in the household projects.

This chapter will give you some ideas of things you can do to help your spouse adjust back to family life, and for your family to adjust to having Dad home.

Common Homecoming Fears and Expectations

As homecoming approaches, all of your family (you, your spouse, and the kids) will have different fears and expectations. While it's good to look forward to homecoming and imagine how it will be, it rarely plays out as you think. Be flexible, go slow, and don't expect anything. That way, you won't be disappointed, and you will probably be pleasantly surprised.

There are some common fears for each family member. Some of them overlap, but others are specific to the perspective of that individual.

These are some fears you may have:

- He will have changed.
- The kids won't remember him or won't accept him.
- I'll lose all independence.
- He's been independent for a while and won't want to be part of the family anymore.
- I won't feel the same way about him as I used to.
- I've put on (or lost) weight and he won't find me attractive anymore.
- I'm going to have to change the routines again.
- The house isn't ready.

These are some fears your spouse may have:

- My family won't need me.
- The kids won't remember me or accept me.
- My marital relationship won't be the same.
- Everyone will have changed.
- There will be no discipline in the household.

These are some fears your kids may have:

♦ Dad won't like me.

♦ I'm going to be in trouble with Dad for bad things I did or low grades I got while he was gone.

♦ Dad isn't going to want to do things with me.

♦ I'm not going to get to continue fun things that I've started doing while Dad was gone.

♦ Everything (routine, etc.) is going to change.

♦ I'll lose some of the responsibilities I've been given while Dad was gone.

Worrying that kids won't remember their Dad or accept him immediately is a valid concern depending on their age. Even if the deployment was only six months, that is a quarter of a two-year-old's lifetime. Young babies may cry and not want to go to Dad. This can be tough for the Dad. Having kept photos and maybe a Daddy Doll near the child during the deployment will help.

Going through family albums as the homecoming approaches can aid the recognition, too. It reminds the children of all the fun things they do with their Dad (particularly things they haven't done with you while he's been gone). This can help them feel excited about seeing Dad and a little less anxious.

Try to introduce Dad as you would an uncle or grandparent who hasn't seen the child for a while. Don't expect Dad to be able to change diapers and such immediately. Let the child get used to seeing her parent first. It shouldn't take long. Your child may remember him clearly right away, but be prepared that it may not be so.

The important thing to realize is that everyone has fears and anxieties about homecoming. It's completely normal and affects all of you. So expect stress levels to be higher, tempers to be a little shorter, and so on. It does not mean that you and the kids are not really excited about your spouse getting home.

> **Top's Tips**
>
> Here are a few tips for a successful reintegration: 1) go slow (don't
> expect everything to be perfect overnight); 2) don't expect everything
> to be as it was before he left; 3) be flexible; 4) be supportive of both
> your spouse and kids; 5) communicate, communicate, communicate! Talk
> to spouse and kids about changes, so that no one is feeling depressed
> or shut out.

The Reintegration Process

Whether or not you have kids, the roles in the household will have
changed while your spouse was gone. He can't be responsible for car
maintenance, etc. when he's in a different country, so you have assumed
that task as well as others you had before.

It's important to talk about roles and responsibilities so that you're on
the same page and know what each other wants to do.

You may really want to hand back all of his previous responsibilities
immediately, or there may be some you don't want to give up. It's possible your spouse doesn't want to do any of it just yet. Alternatively, he
may relish the chance to get back to "normal" tasks. If you do everything for him, he may feel like he's out of place and not needed in the
family.

If you have kids, the transition of tasks involving them should be a bit
more gradual. An immediate change can get them more unsettled, so
if you are returning many responsibilities that involve the kids, do it
gradually, and wherever possible give them the choice of having Dad do
whatever the task is or not.

This process is called reintegration, and it can take up to six months
if he's coming back from a long deployment in a combat zone. Most
people who've been on shorter deployments don't take that long, but
it's important to remember that it takes time, particularly if it was your
spouse's first deployment.

Who Is the Head of the Household Now?

However it worked before your spouse deployed, you have been the head of the household while he has been gone. How you modify this when he returns is entirely up to you and your spouse.

He may want to take over immediately. I would advise against this because it's a bit of a shock to the system for the kids (and you!). Plus, your spouse has only been around military adults for an extended period of time, and may inadvertently expect your children to respond in the same way.

He could have the opposite reaction and feel guilty about having been gone for so long, and therefore spoil the kids. This is a disaster. Kids will learn that Dad will let them do it, so don't ask Mom. He may let them get away with breaking rules, too. This is something you need to discuss with him before it happens.

Explain the rules that have been made while he's gone. They can be modified if you want, but that should be a decision you both make together. Ideally, he will watch how you handle situations and then follow suit. If he doesn't, don't get mad at him (certainly not in front of the kids) but later on, make sure to explain how the rules have been while he's been gone. Then you can both decide if you want to keep it that way or change it.

What happens in most families is Dad takes on some of the more desirable responsibilities and Mom continues the more chore-like ones for a little bit. Then as things get back to normal, the chores will end up distributed more evenly.

Top's Tips

Don't have a list of things for your spouse to do around the house, or immediately expect him to do all the chores he used to do. You've managed perfectly well while he's been gone, so consider the reintegration process as part of the deployment, and don't expect too much of him until he's properly settled. This will help prevent him from getting overwhelmed, or arguments occurring.

Don't expect your spouse to be the sole disciplinarian in the household. For one thing, he may need some peaceful time; anything that could feel like aggression may make him uneasy.

Maintaining the Routine

Some families, particularly those who deal with frequent (but shorter) deployments, have "deployment" and "nondeployment" routines. This can work out well, because kids know what to expect when Dad's gone, and the transition period for when he leaves or comes back becomes far shorter and easier.

> **Top's Tips**
>
> If you have weekly activities that are different for when Dad is home versus deployed, consider having two family weekly calendars— one for deployment one for nondeployment. This can help kids see the differences and be prepared for the changes when you get the alternate calendar out, as you prepare for the deployment or homecoming.

There is a lot of responsibility for the spouse who stayed at home. Many people think that when their spouse returns from deployment, that sole responsibility for the family will go away immediately. It *will* diminish, but rarely as quickly as you might think. You will also become responsible for one more family member (your spouse).

So long as you're aware that this will happen, you are less likely to resent it. The less you resent it, the quicker your spouse will transition, and you'll get to hand over some of the tasks and responsibility.

Managing Stress and Emotional Letdown

Homecoming and reintegration will certainly be different from your expectations. Imagining how it will be is great, and can really help you through homecoming anxiety, but you mustn't expect it to be just as you imagine it.

It's harder for kids to understand this. Whereas you might be a bit disappointed if it isn't as special and magical as you'd expected, your kids' response will be much stronger. They may act up, seem selfish, be mad at Dad (or you), withdraw and seem sad, or a combination of all of these.

Talk with your spouse about plans for the homecoming day before he leaves. He may want a big homecoming party, or he may not. Respect his wishes. Either way, you and the kids can make welcome home signs to put on and in the house.

If he doesn't want a party, don't make plans for after you meet him at the airport or dock. Explain to your kids that Dad will likely be very tired and just want to go home and sleep for a while. That way, if your spouse is bright and bouncy and raring to play with the kids and do stuff, great. But if he's really tired, jetlagged, and just wants to sleep for a few days, you've primed your kids for that response in advance, so they know it's not that Dad doesn't love them and want to spend time with them.

Keep Talking

Communication is the key to a successful reintegration. Don't hide things from your spouse, but be aware of tact when approaching certain subjects.

If he does or says something that hurts your feelings, you need to tell him. Don't let it get to a breaking point where you just start shouting. It's much better to mention it calmly after it happens and explain how it made you feel. Most of the time he won't have realized. Plus, tact doesn't exactly feature highly in their day-to-day lives on deployment. It can take a few gentle prompts to remind him that he's around family now. (The same is true if his language is a bit crude.)

It can be hard for couples, because you've not had the intimacy and close contact for the length of his deployment. You may find that however much you love each other, you need a bit more space than you had anticipated. As with all of this, go slowly without any kind of expectations.

The Uniformed Services University of the Health Sciences' Courage to Care program provides fact sheets on a variety of topics. One of them is specifically for couples' post-deployment. You can get the PDF document directly at www.usuhs.mil/psy/RFSMC.pdf. Other fact sheets in

the Courage to Care program are available at www.usuhs.mil/psy/
courage.html.

Money, Money, Money

One major cause of stress is money. While your spouse was gone, you
probably got around $500–$900 a month more than when he was home.
Hopefully you were saving that, and managed on your pre-deployment
budget. If not, you're going to have to curb some of your spending now,
or things are going to get very tight.

Remember, you can always use the financial counseling from your
branch's nonprofit or through the Family Support Center, to help you
create a budget and help you work out what you will actually be getting post-deployment (after a year or more it can be hard to remember).
Don't forget that you've probably been getting tax-free pay, so you need
to factor that into the equation, too.

Support Resources

Deployments are not much fun at the best of times. But your Family
Support Center and www.militaryonesource.com are both excellent
resources for all stages of deployment and reintegration. You can
get straight to the Military OneSource articles about deployment at
http://tinyurl.com/2rpugr. Another useful resource for tips and links
to branch-specific resources is http://deploymentlink.osd.mil/
deploymentTips.jsp.

What Is PTSD?

Intense stress and traumatic events put a huge strain on people.
Sometimes this develops into Post-Traumatic Stress Disorder (PTSD).
As you might imagine, combat is both intensely stressful and traumatic,
so this is a common trigger.

Some reports claim 17 percent of our service men and women returning
from combat zones are diagnosed with PTSD, others go as high as
30 percent. What is agreed upon is that it generally affects women
more than men, and it affects people who are in actual combat far more
than those who are somewhat detached.

As a spouse, you need to know what to look for regarding PTSD. Effective treatments are available, so the sooner you catch it and your spouse begins treatment, the quicker his recovery.

Some of these signs will be normal for the first few weeks, but if it's continuing and not getting any better, it's worth talking to your spouse about getting evaluated (it may take a while to convince him of that).

Here are some signs of PTSD:

◆ Nightmares or flashbacks, reliving the experience

◆ Sleeplessness

◆ Overreaction to slightly stressful events

◆ Exaggerated overprotectiveness of family and desire to keep them safe

◆ Emotional detachment and numbness

◆ Panic attacks

◆ Loss of appetite

◆ Depression

◆ Prolonged sadness or pessimistic outlook

◆ Jumpiness

◆ Lack of energy

◆ Avoidance of anything that reminds them of the experience (chronically being late to work, lack of socialization with other military friends, etc.)

◆ Lack of focus and poor concentration

◆ Strong irritability

Not everyone has all of these symptoms. But if you start to see many of them occurring, it's worth considering PTSD as a possible cause. Symptoms usually present themselves within six months of the trigger event.

Most military (men in particular) don't want to accept that they have PTSD. Depending on the severity, some will come through it on their own, but others will need professional help. In some severe, untreated cases, PTSD can be the underlying cause of abuse and alcoholism, so don't let it get that far.

If you are unsure what to do or want more information about PTSD, contact your Family Support Center, the American Red Cross, or Military OneSource. Don't forget that Military OneSource is available 24/7 if you need it (the phone number is 1-800-342-9647) and they do have counselors available.

The Least You Need to Know

- Communication is the key to a successful reintegration.

- Don't expect too much from the actual homecoming; then you can be pleasantly surprised.

- Know how much you will be getting paid post-deployment so you don't inadvertently go over budget.

- Make routine changes gradually so your kids (and spouse) have time to settle.

- Don't expect your spouse to jump in where he left off. Give him time and space to adjust.

- Try to be as flexible as you can during the reintegration period. It will make everything a lot easier.

Chapter 14

What If He Is Injured in the Field?

In This Chapter

- ◆ How you will find out
- ◆ How you can visit him at no cost to you
- ◆ What pay changes will occur while he's being treated?
- ◆ Will he go back?
- ◆ Support services for you and him

Injuries and illnesses happen all over the world, but when it's on deployment, it seems far more traumatic. If your spouse gets mildly sick, he'll likely be treated in the nearest facility in-country. Minor illnesses usually only last a few days, so he'll be back to work after that. If it's a minor injury that prevents him from continuing his job, he will more likely be moved to a hospital out of the country. It may be in Europe, or he may be flown back to the States. It does not mean he will be flown back to your location.

Usually you'll find out about this from your spouse, another person in his command, or a Casualty Assistance Calls Officer (we'll talk more about the CACO in the next chapter, but suffice it to say they are specifically trained to help you if your spouse has a severe illness or injury, or worse).

Don't flip out if it's something minor. A fractured ankle or an injured shoulder is not life-threatening. Either could happen during everyday life. If it is more major, then there are support services out there to help support you and your spouse during the rehabilitation.

Rehabilitation, Reassignment, and Fisher House

If the injury is severe enough to warrant his return to the United States, he will likely go to one of the major medical facilities (such as Walter Reed) for treatment and rehabilitation. The likelihood is he will not be sent back to his home station for treatment unless that happens to be near to a hospital specializing in combat injuries.

def•i•ni•tion

Fisher House (www.fisherhouse.org) is a nonprofit organization that provides living accommodation for families to be close to an injured or sick spouse. They are located on the grounds of major military and VA hospitals.

Depending on the illness or injury, and the amount of time he will need treatment and recovery, you may be able to join him and stay at a *Fisher House.*

Currently there are 38 Fisher Houses: 37 in the United States and 1 at Landstuhl Regional Medical Center in Germany. There are 22 more Fisher Houses in design and construction phases. To see a map of all current and in-construction locations, go to http://fisherhouse.org/aboutUs/7_FHmap.pdf.

Each house has from 8 to 21 suites in its 5,000–14,000 square-foot building. The kitchen is shared, as is the living-room facility. There is one manager on salary per location. All of the other people who help there are volunteers.

The houses are not run or maintained by Fisher House—that is the military and VA's responsibility. However, the Fisher House Foundation pays for any "room fees," so it never costs the family staying there anything.

Fisher House also manages another program called Hero Miles. This was originally a way for Americans to donate frequent flyer miles to help servicemembers get home during R&R. It used to be the military member's responsibility to pay for the ticket from where he first entered the United States to wherever he lived. Now the military pays for this cost, so Fisher House took over the program to use donated frequent-flyer miles to bring families to the Fisher House locations to be with their injured or sick spouse.

Flight and accommodation costs are usually the two main barriers preventing families from visiting sick or injured spouses. Fisher House helps cover both so you can get on with the important part of supporting your spouse and family without worrying about the cost.

In 2007, Fisher House helped over 10,000 military families, and saved them a total of $10 million in accommodation costs alone (flights were in addition to this). Since its inception, they have helped 120,000 families, and saved them over $100 million in lodging costs.

In 2007, the average stay was 12 to 14 days. For combat casualties, it was 45 to 60 days. Your spouse may stay at a Fisher House while he's recovering from a combat injury that doesn't require hospitalization but does require frequent treatment and rehabilitation.

 Ask the Chief

Just in case you are interested, you can donate to Fisher House using an allotment from your spouse's pay through the Combined Federal Campaign (CFC).

Pay Changes

We've looked at the additional pays your spouse gets while he is deployed. If he is injured and treated outside of that zone, he may lose some of those pays.

You can see what each of these pays is and who is eligible in Chapter 11, but here I'm just going to explain how it may change if your spouse is medically evacuated out of the combat zone temporarily, or permanently.

Hardship Duty Pay—Location (HDP-L)

If he returns to the combat zone within 30 days, there is no change and he'll get Hardship Duty Pay—Location (HDP-L, also known as SAVE pay) without any lapse. If he's out of the area for over 30 days, it is prorated for the month he left, and then also for the month when he returns. If he doesn't go back to the combat zone, he still gets prorated HDP-L for the month he left.

Hostile Fire Pay/Imminent Danger Pay (HFP/IDP)

This is not a prorated pay, so if your spouse is in the combat zone for one day of that month, he gets the full monthly rate (currently $225). So if he is medically evacuated out of the combat zone on March 2, he will still get the full rate for the entire month of March.

Fire in the Hole!

HFP/IDP does not start again if he is transferred to out-patient status and then later readmitted to the hospital as an in-patient. HFP/IDP ends at the end of the month he first becomes an out-patient.

If he's an in-patient in a hospital, or living at a Fisher House as a recovering combat casualty, he will continue to get HFP/IDP for three months.

The eligibility ends when the three months are up, or when he is transferred to being an out-patient (unless he's in a Fisher House). The month he becomes an out-patient is the last month he will get HFP/IDP until he returns to the combat zone.

The Combat Tax Zone Exclusion (CTZE)

CTZE is what makes your spouse's pay tax-free while he is deployed in a combat zone. If he's medically evacuated, he will continue to get his pay tax-free until the end of that month (because it isn't prorated), but no longer than that, unless he is hospitalized.

While he is an in-patient being treated for something to do with that illness or injury, he is eligible for CTZE for that entire month. This also applies if he is rehospitalized for the same injury later on (up to two years after the injury took place).

CTZE always applies to the full month, so even if he is only readmitted for three days, he is eligible for tax-free pay for that entire month.

Family Separation Allowance (FSA)

This $250-a-month pay only stops if all of your spouse's dependents visit him at the treatment site continuously for over 30 days. So if one of your children (must be your spouse's dependent) only visits for 2 weeks, but you and other children stay for over 30 days, you will still continue to get FSA. Equally, if you all visit, but go home on the twenty-ninth day, you will continue to get FSA. Only if you are all there for over 30 days, will you stop getting FSA.

BAH and BAS

Both BAH and BAS will continue to be paid while your spouse is hospitalized. If he becomes an out-patient, he will be expected to pay for his own meals. While he's in the hospital, his meals will be provided for him.

BAH continues to be paid throughout his treatment, as you must retain your home even if you are staying with him at the treatment site.

Combat-Related Injury and Rehabilitation Pay (CIP)

Your spouse may be eligible for CIP if he is medically evacuated out of a combat zone and is in hospitalized status (either an in-patient or living in a Fisher House or other military-affiliated home, such as the Mologne House at Walter Reed, for continued rehabilitation treatment).

The amount is $430 per month, less the HFP/IDP amount if your spouse is still getting it. So for three months your spouse may get $225 for HFP/IDP and $205 for CIP. It totals up to $430 either way. After he no longer gets HFP/IDP, CIP will revert to the full $430 amount.

Eligibility is a bit complicated. It doesn't start until the calendar month following the month of evacuation. So, if your spouse is evacuated on January 8th, he won't become eligible for CIP until February 1st.

CIP ends when he gets a TSGLI payment, or 30 days have gone by since he was notified of eligibility for a TSGLI payment, or he is no longer in "hospitalized" status (as explained above).

TSGLI Payment

If your spouse's injury was a traumatic one (lost limb, eye, etc.) and he has an SGLI insurance policy, he will receive a one-time lump-sum payment through the TSGLI (traumatic injury protection) rider on his SGLI policy.

As much as you'd rather this injury didn't occur, the additional $25,000–$100,000 can be quite useful if you need to modify your home, etc., to make it easier for him.

The injuries that are considered "traumatic," and the amounts paid for each of them, are available at www.insurance.va.gov/sgliSite/TSGLI/TSGLI.htm (click on Schedule of Payments for Traumatic Losses). On this page you can also link through to the claim form. If you need help, you can call the Office of SGLI directly at 1-800-419-1473.

> **Ask the Chief**
>
> If your spouse suffered a traumatic injury during October 7, 2001, through December 1, 2005, (when TSGLI became mandatory for all SGLI policies), your spouse may be eligible for a retroactive payment. This applies to traumatic injuries sustained in direct support of Operation Enduring Freedom or Operation Iraqi Freedom.

The Wounded Warrior's Handbook (provided by DFAS) goes into more detail about these pay changes. Go to www.dfas.mil/militarypay/woundedwarriorpay.html and click on WW Publications. Click Pay and Entitlement Handbook to download the PDF file.

What Happens Now?

If the physician thinks his injury/illness may make him unfit for duty, he will refer him to a Medical Evaluation Board (MEB). If they agree that he is unfit for duty, it goes on to a Physical Examination Board (PEB). They will make a decision regarding the continuation of your spouse's military career.

Return to Duty—Doing the same job as before the injury/illness, possibly with specific limitations on a medical profile (or limited-duty chit). Alternatively, he may be retrained into another job if he cannot continue his current one, but could do other military jobs.

Medical Separation With or Without Severance Pay—Severance pay is paid when the disability rating is over 30 percent and your spouse has less than 20 years in service (i.e., is not eligible for a medical retirement discharge).

To calculate severance pay, double the basic pay amount and multiply that by the number of years in service (up to 12).

He may also apply for disability compensation from the VA.

Medical Retirement—This is authorized when the injury is permanent and stable (it's not going to change over the next five years), and the disability rating is over 30 percent, or if he has over 20 years in service.

To determine the Retirement Pay, you need to first calculate the Retired Pay Base. This is the average of the highest 36 months of basic pay your spouse received during his career.

Now you need to make two separate calculations. The higher of the two results will be the medical retirement pay your spouse will receive:

◆ Disability Rating (percentage) × Retired Pay Base

◆ Years of Service × 2.5 percent × Retired Pay Base

Temporary Disabled/Retired List (TDRL)—Your spouse will be put on this list if his injury is not "stable" (it may change over the next five years). A MEB and PEB are required within 18 months (usually at 12–18 months). The minimum amount your spouse can receive while on this list is 50 percent of the Retired Pay Base. The maximum time your spouse can remain on the TDRL is five years.

 Ask the Chief

The military and VA may assign your spouse different disability ratings. This is because the military is only concerned with physical fitness to do the military job, whereas the VA considers all injuries, so they are concerned with civilian marketability of your skills and current limitations.

Military OneSource has information about the medical evaluation process at http://tinyurl.com/2ot7na.

Support for You

Dealing with a traumatic injury is devastating for your spouse, but, depending on the injury, it may be just as hard for you.

In severe brain injury cases, spouses usually become the primary caregiver. This is quite a shock to the system if you've always had your spouse to support you, and now you're his sole support.

Even a lost limb can be very difficult to deal with, even though his personality and mental state usually isn't affected. It can still be a difficult adjustment for everyone involved.

The Military Severely Injured Center

The Military Severely Injured Center is here to help you. This was started in 2005 to help severely injured military members reintegrate back to civilian life in their hometowns. It also provides support services for families of severely injured servicemembers.

Ask the Chief

You can reach the Military Severely Injured Center 24/7 at 1-888-774-1361; or from overseas call 0-800-888-0013, press 05, and then enter 1-888-774-1361 (this makes it toll-free). The website is part of Military Homefront (www. militaryhomefront.dod.mil) but can be reached directly at http://tinyurl.com/2wk4px.

The Military Severely Injured Center offers lots of services, many similar to the Family Support Centers (such as financial counseling, education and employment assistance, childcare support, etc.), but these programs are specifically tailored to families of severely injured servicemembers.

The Walter Reed Army Medical Center has a handbook that will help you understand the process from day one, through all the treatment, rehabilitation, and on from there. It is tailored toward the Army (and obviously treatment at Walter Reed); however, much of the information is relevant to everyone.

This book is called Our Hero Handbook. It is a large file (2MB) so it may take a while to download, but it is available at http://tinyurl.com/2t6wmo.

Heroes to Hometowns

This program assists severely injured servicemembers transition back to their hometown civilian life. It provides many types of local assistance, including adapting a home/vehicle to accommodate your spouse, childcare support, help with paying bills, educational and employment assistance, and more.

To learn more about Heroes to Hometowns, go to www.militaryhomefront.dod.mil and then click Heroes to Hometowns in the top left QOL Resources box. Alternatively, you can go directly to http://tinyurl.com/3b6wq5.

Sew Much Comfort

This nonprofit organization truly restores dignity and pride for many injured servicemembers. If your spouse is hospitalized, he is likely stuck in a hospital gown. "Real" clothing doesn't fit over casts and other medical apparatus. This is where Sew Much Comfort (www.sewmuchcomfort.org) comes in. They provide adapted civilian clothing for injured military members free of charge.

The items look like regular civilian clothing, but they are designed for people who are in treatment for severe injuries. They are easier to put on (so your spouse can do it himself) and still have easy access for physical therapy and other treatments and examinations. It's much nicer than a hospital gown, particularly for an extended stay.

If you are interested in becoming part of this program as a volunteer seamstress, you can request the information packet at www.sewmuchcomfort.org (click on Seamstress Info).

Having an injured spouse turns your world upside down. But there are resources out there to help you, so use them. You may find counseling helpful depending on your spouse's injury and his reaction to it.

The Least You Need to Know

◆ Your spouse may continue to get some of the location-specific pays and benefits he received while he was in the combat zone, while he is in "hospitalized" status.

◆ Fisher House provides free accommodation for families to visit injured spouses being treated at major military hospitals. They also provide free plane tickets through the Hero Miles program.

◆ A combat injury does not always mean medical retirement. There are other options that the Physical Examination Board can choose.

◆ The Military Severely Injured Center is available 24/7 at 1-888-774-1361.

◆ Sew Much Comfort provides adapted clothing for severely injured servicemembers free of charge.

Chapter 15

What If He Doesn't Come Back?

In This Chapter

◆ Who tells you and what happens next

◆ Benefits you and your children are entitled to

◆ Burial rights and arrangements

◆ When you have to move out of military housing

◆ Organizations that can help you

This is the ultimate fear of everyone with a deployed loved one. We know that it's not as likely as it was in previous wars, but that doesn't stop us from worrying about the "what ifs."

This is a difficult chapter to write (particularly because my husband is currently deployed), and I'm sure it's just as hard for someone with a deployed spouse to read. I'm outlining this information in as practical a way as I can. I hope that you will never need this information, but sometimes it's worth knowing in advance what would happen, so it's not as hard to comprehend in the tragic event that you do need it.

The Casualty Assistance Calls Officer (CACO)

Your spouse may have asked you who you would like to be present when you are informed of his death. Often it is a friend from the command, or maybe the base chaplain. Whomever you choose needs to be local. They will not wait to tell you because you asked for your friend from a different state to be present and she can't be there for three days.

The person he listed will come to you with the Casualty Assistance Calls Officer (CACO, pronounced Cay-Co) who will be your official link with the military during this difficult time.

Each branch has a slightly different name for this person. (I'm sticking with CACO because three of the branches use this term).

Navy: Casualty Assistance Calls Officer (CACO)

Marine Corps: Casualty Assistance Calls Officer (CACO)

Coast Guard: Casualty Assistance Calls Officer (CACO)

Army: Casualty Assistance Officer (CAO)

Air Force: Casualty Assistance Representative (CAR)

CACOs are specifically trained to help spouses and military families who have lost a loved one in action. The military takes care of its own, and you will not be cast adrift now.

Ask the Chief

The CACO is your stable point of contact. You will have to deal with lots of different people when making arrangements, looking at legal documents, etc. The CACO will usually be present at all of these appointments to help you through the entire process. If you have any questions or concerns, even after all the initial tasks are done, you can always call your CACO.

The primary function of a CACO is to ensure that you receive all of the benefits you are entitled to, and that your spouse's wishes (as set out on his Record of Emergency Data) are followed. The CACO can also put you in contact with support services both national and local to your area.

It's quite likely that you will fulfill three roles: Primary Next of Kin (PNOK), Person Eligible to Receive Personal Effects (PERE), and Person Authorized to Direct Disposition of Remains (PADD). These roles are assigned on your spouse's Record of

Emergency Data, so three different people could fulfill these roles, but it's more likely that you will do all three. The CACO will explain each role and what it means.

The CACO will be available to you when your spouse's Commanding Officer returns his personal effects. He will also schedule (and be present at) your legal appointment to discuss the legal documents your spouse has made (will, estate planning, etc.) and how those will affect the insurance and benefit claims you will file for. He will also assist you in administrative requirements such as getting a new ID card (since your current one is now invalid). Incidentally, you retain Commissary and Exchange privileges.

Each branch of the service has its own website for the Casualty Assistance Office. Some of the publications are not completely up to date, so go with what your CACO says if there is a discrepancy. But this is good information that's worth reading.

Army: www.armycasualty.army.mil

Air Force: www.afcrossroads.com/casualty/main.cfm#

Navy: www.npc.navy.mil/CommandSupport/CasualtyAssistance

Marine Corps: https://www.manpower.usmc.mil/portal/page?_pageid=278,1938196&_dad=portal&_schema=PORTAL (http://tinyurl.com/2ngyba will get you to the same place).

Coast Guard: www.uscg.mil/hq/psc/ras/sbp.asp

There is a really good Department of Defense publication that spells out all of the basic benefits that are available to all branches. It's called "A Survivor's Guide to Benefits—Taking Care of Our Own." You will get a copy from your CACO, but you can also get it online at www.militaryhomefront.dod.mil/survivorsguide. They revise it twice a year, and you can see which version you have by looking at the date on the front cover. As of this writing, the current version was produced February 19, 2008.

I have summarized the benefits here, but I strongly suggest you read this DoD publication cover to cover (it's only 20 pages).

Burial Rights

One of your first responsibilities (assuming you are the Person Authorized to Direct Disposition of Remains, PADD) is your spouse's funeral.

The CACO or Mortuary Officer will assist you in the decisions you will make. Assuming you wish the burial/cremation to take place in the United States, the remains will be flown back with a military escort (usually a member of your spouse's command). You should refrain from setting a funeral date until your spouse's remains have arrived back in the United States, because flight delays/cancellations do happen.

Ask the Chief

All active-duty military may be buried in Arlington National Cemetery or any other National Cemetery.

If you prefer, the military will pay "normal costs" for a private funeral. The amount reimbursed depends on what services are provided. Check with your CACO before making any firm commitments.

The military will pay to transport your spouse's immediate family members to the burial site. This includes you, any dependent children, your parents, and your spouse's parents. They pay for roundtrip transportation as well as two days of per diem for each person. Talk to your CACO before making any travel arrangements to make sure they are all reimbursable.

During the military honors ceremony, any posthumous medals will be awarded, and a folded flag will be presented to both you and your spouse's parents.

Survivor Benefits

Wondering how you and the kids will cope financially can be a major concern, particularly if you relied upon your spouse's income. There are various survivor benefits that your CACO will help you apply for.

Death Gratuity and Unpaid Pay

Your spouse can designate one or more beneficiaries to receive the death gratuity and unpaid pay/allowances due. This is done in 10 percent increments. The likelihood is this will come to you, or it may be shared with any children you have.

The death gratuity is $100,000 tax-free and is paid if your spouse died while on active-duty or within 120 days of discharge, provided his death was due to a service-related injury/illness. This is usually paid within 72 hours (3 days), and comes from the Department of Defense.

Any pay and benefits that are due to your spouse will also be paid to this same beneficiary.

 Ask the Chief _____

If you live in military housing, you do not have to move out right away. You are allowed to stay in military housing for a full year. If you live off-base you will receive one year's worth of BAH as a lump sum. If you move out of base housing, you will receive a lump sum of BAH prorated for the rest of the year.

Dependency and Indemnity Compensation (DIC)

This flat-rate monthly payment is available to families of active-duty members who died from a service-related injury/illness (as determined by the VA, who pays this benefit).

This is a fixed monthly amount that goes up every year to compensate for cost-of-living increases. For 2008, the rate for a surviving spouse is $1,091. For each unmarried dependent child under 18 (23 if attending a VA approved college full-time) there is an additional $271 per month.

Receiving DIC benefits is not automatic. You have to apply to

 Ask the Chief _____

If you have children under 18, you will receive an extra $250 per month for the first two years you are eligible for DIC. This is called Transition Assistance and will stop either when the two years are up, or when your children are no longer minors.

the VA for it. It's also tax-free, so it's usually worth doing, but talk to your CACO about your options as it does affect the amount you will get from the Survivor Benefits Plan.

Survivor Benefits Plan (SBP)

This benefit is provided by the Department of Defense. If your spouse dies on active-duty, you are entitled to 55 percent of what his retirement pay would have been if he'd been medically retired at 100 percent disabled.

I explained how to calculate medical retirement pay in Chapter 14, so refer back to determine the amount.

Payments under the Survivor Benefits Plan are not tax-free. Also, the eligible amount is reduced by any amount you receive for Dependency and Indemnity Compensation (DIC) from the VA.

There are ways to maximize your benefits; this can include opting for a child-only benefit for DIC. Before you make any decisions, talk to your CACO and the retirement services officer you will be referred to.

SGLI

If your spouse had an SGLI policy, the beneficiary (usually you) will receive the payout (up to $400,000) usually within 45 days.

TSGLI

The SGLI beneficiary may also receive a payment for TSGLI if your spouse sustained an injury that would qualify him for a TSGLI payment, and he survived for seven days after the injury. TSGLI payments range from $25,000 to $100,000.

TRICARE and TRICARE Dental Coverage

TRICARE coverage for you and your children will continue for three years exactly as you had it while he was active-duty. You are eligible for all of the same policies during this time.

During these three years, you will be referred to as a "Transitional Survivor." After the three years are up, you become a "Survivor." At that point, you will have to pay for TRICARE coverage, but it will be at the retiree rates (these are still just a fraction of what you would otherwise pay for health-care insurance).

 Ask the Chief _____

If your spouse was a reservist or National Guard, so long as he was active-duty for over 30 days before he died, you are eligible for all active-duty policies for three years.

When you become a "Survivor" you will no longer be eligible for the overseas or remote TRICARE policies (see Chapter 1). However, any unmarried children under 21 (23 if in full-time education) will remain in "Transitional Survivor" status until they are no longer eligible for TRICARE.

TRICARE Dental works in a similar way. For the first three years, you will be part of the TRICARE Survivor Benefits Plan. After that, you can choose to transfer your policy to the TRICARE Retiree Dental Program. There are premiums associated with this plan type, which vary by location, so go to www.trdp.org/pro/premiumSrch.html to determine your rate.

Dependents' Educational Assistance (DEA)

Surviving spouses and children (including step- and adopted children) are eligible for the Dependents' Educational Assistance (DEA) benefit from the VA.

This can be used for a variety of educational programs including undergraduate and graduate degree, certificate program, apprenticeship, on-the-job training, SAT (and other college entrance exams), and CLEP. Surviving spouses may also get DEA benefits for correspondence (distance education) courses. All of the authorized program types are available at www.gibill.va.gov/GI_Bill_Info/programs.htm.

The VA must approve the specific institution. You can search for approved colleges, universities, and other educational facilities at http://inquiry.vba.va.gov/weamspub/buildSearchInstitutionCriteria.do.

The benefits are for 45 months total, but they do not have to be consecutive, and you may not be charged a full month's benefit if you're attending part-time or using distance education.

DEA Payment Rates Effective October 1, 2007

Attendance	Monthly Benefit Maximum
Full Time	$881.00
¾ Time	$661.00
½ Time	$439.00
Less Than ½, But More Than ¼ Time	$439.00
¼ Time	$220.28

The rates change every year, so go to www.gibill.va.gov/GI_Bill_Info/rates.htm, scroll down to the DEA section, and click on the most current date to see the rates that will apply to you (it usually changes in October).

DEA eligibility for children is from age 18 to 26, and it doesn't matter if they get married during that time. However, if your child begins to get DEA benefits, he will lose any DIC benefit you may have been paid for him.

Because DIC ends at age 23, it might be better for your child to defer DEA benefits until after DIC stops and then use her DEA benefits for the remaining years of study, or for a graduate degree. That way you get to maximize both benefits. This is certainly something to discuss with a VA specialist.

For surviving spouses (assuming your spouse died while on active-duty), the DEA benefit is valid for 20 years from your spouse's death. If you remarry before age 57, DEA eligibility ends and all benefits will stop. If you remarry after age 57, your DEA eligibility will be unaffected.

You apply for DEA benefits directly with the VA in your state. If you've already started the education program, you can still apply for DEA benefits, but it is a different form to submit, so make sure you get the right one.

Supporting You and Your Family

This is a very difficult time for you and your family. You do have support through the military, but there are other organizations who are also there to help you.

TAPS

TAPS stands for Tragedy Assistance Program for Survivors. It is a nonprofit organization that helps military families cope with the loss of their loved one. It is not a government program, nor do they receive any government funding.

TAPS (www.taps.org) offers many support programs and seminars including the following:

◆ Good grief camps and seminars (to attend with other people in a similar situation)

◆ One-to-one peer support (they call it "companioning")

◆ Help with traumatic loss and grief

◆ Online forums and scheduled "chat" times for specific age groups

TAPS is a wonderful organization and one I wholeheartedly support. I strongly recommend any surviving spouses (and children) make use of their programs. You can contact them 24/7 at 1-800-959-TAPS.

 Ask the Chief

TAPS is an appropriate name for this organization, because Taps is also the name of the evocative bugle call sounded at military funerals, memorials, and wreath-laying ceremonies.

Bereavement Counseling

Your Family Support Center offers counseling services, but you can also contact the VA office of Readjustment Counseling Service (RCS) who provide bereavement counseling for surviving spouses and children of active-duty military. You can contact this VA office at 202-273-9116.

Gold Star Wives of America

At (or before) your spouse's funeral, you will have been given the Gold Star Lapel Button. This may seem strange to you, but this lapel pin is only authorized by Congress for surviving families of active-duty military, or military veterans who died of a service-related disability. It's entirely up to you if you want to wear it or not. All immediate family members will be presented with the pin.

This explains the name of the Gold Star Wives of America (www. goldstarwives.org). This nonprofit organization is only for spouses (female or male) who have been presented the Gold Star Lapel Button. There is a membership fee, but it's only $25 per year. Currently there are 10,000 members around the country.

Gold Star Wives is a support service, but also an information source. They will keep you updated on the services available to you, legislation changes, etc. They can also identify any state-specific benefits you are eligible for. They send out quarterly newsletters to keep you updated.

There are local chapters across the country. To find your closest one, go to www.goldstarwives.org/regions-chapters.htm.

The Gold Star Wives website has a comprehensive list of other organizations, scholarships, and resources available to surviving military families. Some are specific to the conflict your spouse died in (OIF, OEF, etc.), but this is all clearly separated. To view these resources, go to www.goldstarwives.org/resources-military-family.htm.

Society of Military Widows (SMW)

This is similar to Gold Star Wives, but on a smaller scale. There are not as many chapters around the country, but the dues are lower ($12). Unlike Gold Star Wives, you are only eligible for membership provided you do not remarry. Eligible members are surviving spouses of active-duty, retired, or military who died from a service-related disability.

SMW (www.militarywidows.org) provides support and referral services. They also lobby congress for changes that benefit surviving military spouses.

Snowball Express and Operation Ensuring Christmas

Both Snowball Express and Operation Ensuring Christmas are non-profit organizations that aim to provide some positive memories for surviving children. Snowball Express (www.snowballexpress.org) provides an all-expenses trip for the children (and surviving parent) to a three-day event in Southern California, which ends with a day at Disneyland. This event is usually held at the end of November. They receive lots of gifts during the event, donated by major corporate sponsors.

Snowball Express is a great program because it enables the kids to socialize with other kids just like them. In 2007, Snowball Express sent over 1000 kids to the event.

Operation Ensuring Christmas (www.opchristmas.org) provides a $100 gift card to each child. This can be used by the parent ahead of Christmas to get the gifts on the child's list, or the child can use the gift card himself. Each gift card comes with a personalized Christmas card and two or three notes from donors to the program (examples can be read at www.opchristmas.org/donor-sentiments.php).

Operation Ensuring Christmas also has a Christmas-in-July program where they send kids on a "VIP Vacation" to Orlando, Florida, and to either Disney World or Universal Studios.

Both organizations aim to help kids be "kids" again.

I hope that you were reading this chapter as "what if" information, not because you have lost your spouse. My condolences go out to all spouses and families who are dealing with this firsthand. These support networks and benefits are there specifically to help you, so please utilize them.

The Least You Need to Know

- ◆ The CACO will help you with all the initial decisions, benefits, paperwork, etc. He or she is your military point of contact.
- ◆ Financial benefits are available through the DoD, VA, and others.

- Your military housing benefits do not end immediately. If you live off-base, you will get a lump-sum payment for one-year's worth of BAH. If you live on-base, you can stay there for a year, or move off-base and receive a lump sum for BAH prorated for the rest of the year.

- The military will pay for your spouse's funeral, and also to transport you, your children, and both sets of parents to the burial site, and also for two days of per diem.

- There are various education benefits and scholarships specifically for surviving spouses and children.

- TAPS (www.taps.org) is dedicated to helping surviving spouses and children adjust and learn to cope without their loved one.

Chapter 16

Planning for Retirement ... at 37

In This Chapter

- ◆ Your final PCS move
- ◆ Planning for the future
- ◆ How retirement pay is calculated
- ◆ Benefits you will retain
- ◆ Health care and life insurance for retirees

Retiring at 37 might sound crazy, but if your spouse joined at 17, he will meet the 20 years of minimum service for retirement benefits at 37. He may choose to stay in longer, and, as you will see, the retirement pay gets higher, the longer he serves.

Some of the benefits you are currently getting he will retain, some will have restrictions and limitations once he retires, and some will go away entirely. Preparing for the change will make the adjustment much smoother and easier.

Home of Record Move

The military will pay to move you back to your spouse's Home of Record (HOR). This is where your spouse lived when he signed up.

Many people confuse the Home of Record with the State of Residency. The latter is where he pays taxes. Often they are the same state, however, he can change his State of Residency if he wants to. The HOR does not change.

If you wish to be moved somewhere other than your spouse's Home of Record (which is quite often the case), the military will pay only as much as it would have cost to move you to your spouse's HOR. Quite often it doesn't cost more, but it all depends on your chosen destination. Still, it's a whole lot cheaper and less hassle than funding it all yourself.

Choosing where to go may be influenced by where extended family lives, or by job opportunities, so it's worth thinking about this well in advance of his retirement date.

What Will Your Spouse Do After Retirement?

Many military retirees joke that they're done with work. They're retired now, right? Well, not quite. Later in this chapter we'll look at the financial benefits you retain. While they're good, they're not close to what your family has been used to.

Most of the time, the military member starts another career after leaving the military. Unfortunately, many people are not proactive about it. They're counting down until retirement, but not looking past it. So they end up retired, with a lot less pay coming in, and no future career plans.

Ideally, your spouse should be planning what he wants to do after he retires a few years before that time actually arrives. That way he has time for college courses, etc., and has a clear plan of what is next for him.

If he doesn't have a job lined up to start after retiring, you may lose the benefit of the HOR move. Think about it—the military moves you to Florida because that's your spouse's Home of Record and you didn't request to go elsewhere. Then three months later (after the "retirement novelty" has worn off) he realizes that he really does need a job. Unfortunately, he discovers that to do a job he has the skills for, he has to move to Virginia. The military will not pay for you to move again, so this time it's all up to you to arrange and fund the move.

It's much better to plan ahead and get job offers before deciding where the military will move you for the final time. Your spouse can specify that he's taking three or six months off after retirement (often they like to do this) and then have the job lined up to start after that period of downtime has ended.

From Seasoned Spouses

I know way too many people who have retired from the military, and end up working minimum-wage jobs because they didn't look at the job opportunities and didn't complete college before they got out. They have to take "a job" rather than one they really would like to do because the family needs the money. This can be a hard cycle to get out of, and can be demoralizing for someone who has held an important job in the military.

Thankfully, the military has programs in place to help your spouse adjust to civilian life and plan for what's next.

Transition Assistance Program (TAP)

The Transition Assistance Program is a three-day course for military members leaving the service. It is designed to help them look past their End of Service (EOS) date and plan for the future. They will help with resumés, job applications, translating military skills into civilian language that HR departments will understand, decisions about relocation, etc.

The DoD, VA, and Department of Labor have collaborated to create the TAP website (www.turbotap.org). It is full of information for transitioning back to civilian life. You have to register for the site, but you can download a guide for active-duty retirees or for Reserve/National Guard from the homepage without registering. Another useful website that helps with job searches is www.taonline.com. There is a lot of other useful information on this site, too.

Retirement Pay

This is more complicated than most people think. Most people think that retirement pay is half their basic pay on the day they retire. This is not the case. The rules are different if your spouse entered the military before September 1980, between September 1980 and August 1986, or after August 1986. Decisions he made earlier in his career can also affect the amount he receives, as will how much time he actually has in service.

Calculating the Multiplier

First, you need to calculate your spouse's *multiplier.*

def•i•ni•tion

A **multiplier** is the percentage of basic pay that your spouse will receive for retirement pay.

This is very simple, just multiply his years of service by 2.5. The number you come up with is the multiplier, and is a percentage. So if your spouse has 24 years of service, his multiplier is $24 \times 2.5 = 60$ percent.

This percentage is used in the retirement pay calculation regardless of which formula is used.

Final Pay—If your spouse joined the military before September 8, 1980, the multiplier is multiplied by the basic pay portion of his last paycheck (not including incentive pay or allowances). This amount is what he will receive for retirement pay.

High-3—If your spouse entered the service after September 8, 1980, but before August 1, 1986, your spouse will receive retirement pay based on the High-3 system.

The difference between Final Pay and High-3 is in how they determine the basic pay amount. In Final Pay it is whatever he got in his last paycheck, but with High-3 it is the average of your spouse's highest 36 months (3 years) of basic pay. So yearly pay increases, promotions, and so on, do come into play.

REDUX—This option only applies if your spouse entered the military after August 1, 1986. At 15 years of service, your spouse has the choice of continuing as normal, and retiring under the High-3 system, or entering the REDUX system.

Under the REDUX system, your spouse receives a lump-sum of $30,000 at 15 years of service (called a Career Status Bonus, or CSB). This may seem wonderful at the time, but it has a serious impact on how his retirement pay is calculated later on (plus it is taxable at the lump-sum rate which is currently 25 percent).

Under REDUX you must deduct one percentage point from the multiplier for every year under 30 years of service that your spouse had when he retired. So, let's look at the difference in the multiplier calculation for retirement at 20 years under High-3 and REDUX.

High-3: 2.5×20 years = 50

High-3 multiplier = 50 percent

REDUX: 2.5×20 years = 50

Deduction: 30 years – 20 years = 10

50 – 10 = 40

REDUX multiplier = 40 percent

Because this individual retired at 20 years, he had 10 years' worth of percentage points to deduct from his multiplier. Thus, he only gets 40 percent of basic pay for retirement.

That's quite a difference, but it doesn't end there. All retirees get an annual Cost Of Living (COL) payment. Under the REDUX system, this COL is reduced by 1 percent. Currently the COL is 2.3 percent of your retirement pay, so for people under the REDUX system, it is reduced to 1.3 percent.

Ask the Chief

All of the deductions for REDUX end at age 62, but if your spouse retires at 40 with 20 years in, that's 22 years of getting 10 percent lower pay and 1 percent lower COL. Only you can decide if that $30,000 bonus is worth those deductions later on.

Personally, my gut feeling is that the REDUX option is not worth it, except in specific circumstances:

◆ You have severe financial difficulties and that $30,000 would fix them (and you have a strict plan in place so that you won't get in that situation again).

◆ Your spouse will retire relatively close to the 62-year-old end of benefit reductions.

◆ Your spouse plans to serve significantly more than 20 years. If your spouse serves for 30 years, there is no deduction other than the 1 percent of the annual COL.

◆ You plan to invest the money and the return on investment would exceed the amount you will lose in retirement pay.

In the table that follows, you can see how the difference in percentage used to compute retirement pay gets less, the closer to 30 years in service your spouse gets.

Comparison of Basic Pay Percentage Received Under High-3 and REDUX Systems

Years in Service	High-3	REDUX
20	50%	40%
22	55%	47%
24	60%	54%
26	65%	61%
28	70%	68%
30	75%	75%
34	85%	85%
40	100%	100%

If your spouse is Army or Air Force, and was cited for Extraordinary Heroism (EH), he will receive a 10 percent boost to his multiplier. This is capped at 75 percent, so if your spouse is eligible for more based on time in service, they can just ignore the EH so that he can receive the higher amount.

Retirement calculators are available at www.defenselink.mil/ militarypay/retirement/calc/index.html for each retirement system. In the REDUX calculator, they assume you're investing that $30,000, not spending it.

Thrift Savings Plan (TSP)

If your spouse has been paying into a TSP fund, he can make a number of choices regarding this money after he retires.

◆ Withdraw it all

◆ Withdraw a single payment and leave the rest in the TSP

◆ Receive monthly, or yearly, payments

◆ Have the TSP purchase an annuity for him

There are rules for different situations, so check www.tsp.gov/uniserv/ features/chapter13.html to see all the specifics. Your spouse has to withdraw it in one of these four ways by age 70½.

Other Benefits You Will Keep

You won't get BAH or BAS anymore, however, you will still have on-base privileges. So you can use the gym, family support services, shop in the Commissary and Exchange, etc. All veterans (even those who separate from the military prior to 20 years of service) retain their VA loan eligibility. You can also use the childcare system, but you are the lowest priority now, so the chance of getting a place is very slim.

The biggest benefit you will retain is health care. It's not the same as when your spouse was active-duty, but it's a lot cheaper than civilian health-care plans.

TRICARE for Retirees

Until age 65, you are eligible for the same plans as you were before you retired. However, enrollment fees, co-pays, and deductibles may apply.

If you continue with TRICARE Prime, you will pay an annual enrollment fee (currently $230 individual or $460 for the entire family). This is very reasonable, because many civilian health-care plans charge this per month, not per year.

So long as you continue to receive care at Military Treatment Facilities, you won't pay deductibles. If you choose to seek out-of-network (called Point of Service) care, you pay an annual deductible of $300 for individual or $600 for family plans.

If you don't want to pay an enrollment fee, you can go with TRICARE Standard and Extra, but when you use civilian services, the co-pays are much higher. The deductibles for TRICARE Standard and Extra are $150 for individual and $300 for family.

You can compare the plans at www.tricare.mil/mybenefit/home/overview/ComparePlans. Remember, you're looking for retiree information, not active-duty or reserve.

TRICARE For Life

To be eligible for TRICARE For Life you must have both Medicare Part A and Part B. TRICARE pays secondary to Medicare, so in many situations you'll have no out-of-pocket cost (other than the Medicare Part B coverage).

The cost for Medicare Part B is determined by your gross annual income. You can find the current rates at www.medicare.gov. (Click on FAQs and then select Medicare Part B Monthly Premiums in 2008. The year will be whatever the current year is.) In 2008 the rates range from $96.40 to $238.40 per month.

Here are some highlights of the TRICARE For Life policy:

- ◆ You can use any Medicare approved provider.
- ◆ In most cases there are no claims to file. Your provider will bill Medicare, and they will forward the claim to TRICARE if there is any fee still outstanding.

◆ No enrollment fee from TRICARE (you only pay for the Part B coverage through Medicare).

◆ Catastrophic Cap (the maximum you will pay per year) is $3,000.

If only TRICARE covers the service, the deductible is $150 for individual and $300 for family plans. If only Medicare covers it, then Medicare deductibles apply. If both cover the service, then you do not have a deductible.

You may have a co-pay depending on whether both, or just one of the companies covers the service (as shown in the table).

Co-Pay for Medical Services Under TRICARE For Life

Service Covered By ...	Your Co-Pay
Both Medicare and TRICARE	$0
Medicare Only	Medicare cost-share applies
TRICARE Only: In-Network	20% after deductible is met
TRICARE Only: Out-of-Network	25% after deductible is met

These cost-shares apply to out-patient, clinical preventative, emergency, and out-patient behavioral health-care services. Hospitalization, in-patient behavioral health-care, and in-patient skilled nursing care all have different co-pays.

TRICARE Retiree Dental Program (TRDP)

In Chapter 14, I covered the TRICARE Dental Program for retirees. It's the same if your spouse is retired for disability or for time in service. You are still eligible for the TRICARE Retiree Dental Program (TRDP) if you are over 65.

The TRDP is provided by Delta Dental. The cost varies by the region you live in. To find the cost, go to www.trdp.org/pro/premiumSrch. html and enter your zip code.

For more information about this program, go to www.trdp.org/pro/ overview.html. This webpage has an excellent overview including benefits, co-pays, eligibility, and more.

Veterans' Group Life Insurance (VGLI)

If your spouse has an SGLI policy, he can convert it to VGLI (Veterans' Group Life Insurance) within one year and 120 days of retiring. This is a renewable Term Life insurance policy.

SGLI covers your spouse for the first 120 days after leaving the military, so VGLI will kick in on day 121 if he enrolls any time within that first 120-day period.

He can obtain VGLI for $10,000 to $400,000 (in $10,000 increments), but it can't be higher than his previous SGLI policy was. So if you want a $400,000 policy but have a lower amount currently, he needs to increase his SGLI to $400,000 before he retires.

The premium cost for VGLI is based on age and the amount of coverage. Go to www.insurance.va.gov/sgliSite/VGLI/VGLI.htm and click VGLI Premium Rates to see all the rates. Your spouse can keep VGLI for the rest of his life if he wants to.

Top's Tips

If you have any concerns about your spouse's health, make sure he gets this conversion done ASAP. If he does it within 120 days of retiring, he doesn't have to have a medical examination to show good health. If it's after 120 days, he must submit evidence that he's in good health.

Fire in the Hole!

There is no family version of VGLI, so you will need to convert your FSGLI policy to a commercial one, or it will lapse and you will have no life insurance coverage for yourself.

When Your Spouse Can Be Recalled to Active-Duty

Any prior active-duty member can be recalled to active-duty after retirement—even if he was retired on medical disability (although this is unlikely).

Fleet Reserve

Navy and Marine Corps retirees are transferred to the Fleet Reserve (or Marine Corps Fleet Reserve) until their time in service plus time since retirement reaches 30 years.

Until that time, they receive "retainer" pay rather than retirement pay. It's the same amount, and all of the other benefits are the same. The only difference is that they can be involuntarily recalled to active-duty. So these retirees would be the first to be recalled.

After 30 years total service (including any time in Fleet Reserve), your spouse is transferred to retired status. He can still be recalled, but the restrictions that apply to the other branches at 20 years of service then apply.

On the Retired List

There are three categories of retirees. Category one is more likely to get recalled to active-duty than category two, and so on.

Category 1: Retired for less than five years, nondisabled, under 60 years old.

Category 2: Retired for over five years, nondisabled, under 60 years old.

Category 3: All other retirees (including those over 60 years old and disabled).

Once your spouse is on the retired list, the only way he can be recalled is if Congress declares a State of War or National Emergency. At this point, the Secretary of Defense can then authorize the Secretaries of each individual branch to recall retired military personnel to active-duty.

Without a law change, this is the only way your spouse can be recalled. Even if the Secretary of Defense gives this authorization, it doesn't mean it will actually happen.

Retired military personnel do get a lot of benefits (far more than our civilian counterparts), but it pays to plan ahead and know what to expect. For more information about veteran benefits, contact www.va.gov.

The Least You Need to Know

- The military will pay to move you to your spouse's Home of Record, or pay up to that cost if you want to be moved elsewhere.

- Don't let retirement sneak up on you. Have a clearly defined plan of where you're going after retirement.

- Retirement pay is calculated based on your spouse's Multiple and (usually) highest 36 months of basic pay.

- REDUX looks like a good deal at 15 years, but it may not be the best long-term plan for your spouse if he plans to retire at 20 years, not later.

- SGLI can be converted to VGLI but there is no family equivalent.

- You are eligible for TRICARE after retirement, but you may pay a premium, or co-pays, depending on the plan.

Appendix A

Glossary

Basic Allowance for Housing (BAH)   A nontaxable, monthly allowance provided instead of government quarters. The rate is based on your local rental market.

Basic Allowance for Subsistence (BAS)   A monthly, flat-rate, nontaxable allowance for food.

Career Status Bonus (CSB)   The $30,000 bonus your spouse receives at 15 years if he chooses the REDUX retirement plan.

Child Development Center (CDC)   A daycare facility run by the DoD for military children at subsidized rates.

Child Development Homes (CDH)   In-home childcare licensed and subsidized by the DoD. CDH is a Navy term. It is the same program as Family Child Care (FCC).

Child and Youth Registration and Referral   Assists military families with locating childcare services in their local area.

Clothing Allowance   Paid yearly to help offset the cost of replacing uniforms and boots, having new patches sewn onto uniforms, etc. The rate varies by branch of service and gender.

CONUS   Stands for Continental United States. It is used to distinguish between programs and benefits for people stationed within the United States versus overseas.

Cost of Living Allowance (COLA)   An allowance to help offset the cost of living in high-priced areas. Overseas, it's called OCOLA.

Defense Finance and Accounting Service (DFAS)   The DoD department responsible for paying your spouse.

Dislocation Allowance (DLA)   Helps cover the costs associated with a PCS move that are not otherwise covered by other allowances.

Family Readiness Group (FRG)   A command-level group that helps support the spouses and families of deployed servicemembers from that unit command.

Family Separation Allowance (FSA)   Paid when your spouse is deployed or stationed away from you.

Family Child Care (FCC)   In-home childcare that is licensed and subsidized by the DoD. Same as Child Development Homes (CDH).

High-3   How retirement pay is calculated for most active-duty (not using REDUX). The amount paid is a percentage of the average of the highest 36 months of basic pay your spouse has received.

Individual Rate Protection   Guarantees that your monthly BAH allowance won't go down if your local BAH rate decreases.

M&IE   This stands for Meals and Incidental Expenses and is part of your TLE payment. The allowance varies based on location and the number of people (and their ages) in your family.

Move-In Housing Allowance (MIHA)   A one-time payment to help pay for expenses incurred when moving into private housing overseas to make the accommodation habitable. For example, you might use it for purchasing space heaters or wardrobes.

Multiplier   The percentage of basic pay that your spouse will receive for retirement pay. It is calculated by multiplying your spouse's number of years in service by 2.5.

No-Cost TDY/TAD Orders   Orders that give the military member time off without charging the time to his leave balance. It is used for certain elective schools (such as if the person wanted to go to Jump School and get parachute qualified), but is most commonly used for house-hunting leave when you PCS.

O-CONUS Stands for Outside Contiguous United States. It refers to stations overseas or in Alaska or Hawaii.

On The Economy A phrase used to refer to anything you do off-base in an overseas location. For example, *living on the economy* means living off-base; *working on the economy* means working off-base.

Overseas Housing Allowance (OHA) Covers the majority of your living expenses, including moving-in allowance, utilities, and rent, if you live in nongovernment housing overseas.

Per Diem A monetary allowance paid daily for lodging, food, and incidental expenses while you are PCSing, your spouse is traveling on TAD/TDY orders, or is deployed.

Permanent Change of Station (PCS) A change of duty station. This is different from a TAD/TDY or a deployment because your whole family is moved (assuming the orders are accompanied).

Power of Attorney (POA) A document giving the named person authority to make legal decisions on behalf of the grantor.

REDUX A retirement plan chosen at 15 years of service. It provides an immediate $30,000 taxable bonus, but then the servicemember receives a lower amount of retirement pay and COLA based on how many years of service he had when he retired.

Rental Ceiling The maximum monthly allowance for overseas housing. If you use less than the maximum, you are only paid the exact amount you use. If you pay more, you receive the maximum allowance.

Rest and Recuperation (R&R) Two weeks time off authorized for most people on a 270 day deployment or longer. It's not guaranteed, though, so be very happy if you get it.

Selective Reenlistment Bonus (SRB) A bonus paid to enlisted servicemembers in specific jobs as a reenlistment incentive.

Servicemember Group Life Insurance (SGLI) Life insurance for military members which can be converted to a veteran's policy (VGLI) after they retire. Family version is called FSGLI.

Temporary Lodging Allowance (TLA) Same principle as TLE, but used if you are overseas. It is paid for up to 60 days. The amount is determined by the location.

Temporary Lodging Expense (TLE)   Pays for 10 days of hotel expenses; can be used at the departing duty station, at the new duty station, or in any combination. The amount is determined by the zip code of the duty station.

Transportation Office (TO)   Also known as Personal Property Office (PPO) and Transportation Management Office (TMO). They help you arrange your household goods shipment.

TRICARE   The military health-care insurance provider.

Unaccompanied Baggage (UB)   The air shipment of your household goods when moving to or from overseas locations. The weight allowance is low and it is strictly for essential items only.

United Concordia   The insurance company that provides the TRICARE Dental Program.

Utility/Recurring Maintenance Allowance   A monthly allowance for overseas families living in nongovernment housing to help pay for the utility expenses.

VA Loan   A home loan through a traditional lender that is guaranteed by the government. You usually get lower interest rates and are not required to have a deposit payment.

Vehicle Registration Office (VRO)   On overseas bases the VRO will help you with vehicle licensing issues for vehicles you bring into the country or buy while you're there; they'll also make sure you follow the right regulations for shipping it back to the United States.

Volunteer Income Tax Assistance (VITA)   Volunteers who will help you prepare your taxes. The office is usually on-base and manned by both active-duty and civilian volunteers.

Appendix B

Quick Reference

Throughout the book, I have referred to many websites. To make it easier for you, I've put it all together here for quick reference.

Military Websites

Official Websites For Military Families In Each Branch

Branch	Official Site	Family Site	Charity
Army	www.army.mil	www.armyfamiliesonline.org	www.aerhq.org
Air Force	www.af.mil	www.afcrossroads.com	www.afas.org
Navy	www.navy.mil	www.lifelines.navy.mil	www.nmcrs.org
Marine Corps	www.usmc.mil	www.lifelines.navy.mil	www.nmcrs.org
Coast Guard	www.uscg.mil		www.cgmahq.org
Army National Guard	www.ngb.army.mil	www.guardfamily.org	
Air National Guard	www.ang.af.mil	www.guardfamily.org	

MilitaryHOMEFRONT
www.militaryhomefront.dod.mil

Military OneSource
www.militaryonesource.com
1-800-342-9647 (phone line manned 24/7)

Employment and Education Resources

Family, Employment, and Education Information
www.milspouse.org

Military Spouse Career Center
www.military.com/spouse

Servicemember Opportunity College (SOC)
www.soc.aascu.org (click on the branch of service on the left sidebar for branch specific information).

Pay Tables and Allowances

Basic Pay
www.dfas.mil/militarypay/militarypaytables.html

BAH Calculator
http://perdiem.hqda.pentagon.mil/perdiem/bah.html

CONUS and OCONUS Per Diem Calculator
http://perdiem.hqda.pentagon.mil/perdiem/perdiemrates.html

CONUS COLA Calculator
http://perdiem.hqda.pentagon.mil/perdiem/ccform.html

OCONUS COLA Calculator
http://perdiem.hqda.pentagon.mil/perdiem/ocform.html

Travel Pay Information
http://perdiem.hqda.pentagon.mil

SGLI and FSGLI Information
www.insurance.va.gov

Childcare Services and Subsidies

Locate Child Development Centers
www.militaryinstallations.dod.mil

Army Child and Youth Services
www.armymwr.com/portal/family/childandyouth

Marine Corps Child Development Center
www.usmc-mccs.org/cyt/cdc.cfm

Navy Child and Youth Programs
https://qol.persnet.navy.mil/CYPWeb/Web/Home/Home.aspx

Air Force Child Development Programs
http://public.afsv.net/FMP/ChildProgramsDotCom/CDC.htm

Coast Guard Child Development Centers
www.uscg.mil/hq/g-w/g-wk/wkw/child_care/child_development_
centers.htm

Child Care Aware
www.childcareaware.org
1-800-424-2246

Operation Military Child Care
www.naccrra.org/MilitaryPrograms/program.php?Page=11

Military Child Care In Your Neighborhood
www.naccrra.org/MilitaryPrograms/program.php?Page=12

Relocation Resources (other than Family Support Center)

How to Ship a Vehicle Overseas
www.sddc.army.mil/sddc/Content/Pub/8808/DBCN8808.pdf

Military Teens on the Move (MTOM)
www.defenselink.mil/mtom

Information for moving kids
www.cfs.purdue.edu/mfri/pages/moving_website/kids_brochure.pdf

Military Child Education Coalition
www.militarychild.org

Deployment Assistance

Courage to Care Fact Sheets
www.usuhs.mil/psy/courage.html

Branch Specific Tips for Deployments
http://deploymentlink.osd.mil/deploymentTips.jsp

What to expect during R&R
http://tinyurl.com/2lsmu8 (on Military OneSource)

Deployment Resource Guides and Articles
http://tinyurl.com/2rpugr (on Military OneSource)

Injury and Survivor Benefit Information

DFAS Wounded Warrior Entitlements Handbook
www.dfas.mil/army2/woundedinaction/WWEHandbook_Web_062607.
pdf

A Survivor's Guide to Benefits (DoD publication)
www.militaryhomefront.dod.mil/survivorsguide

TSGLI Schedule of Payments and Claims Form
www.insurance.va.gov/sgliSite/TSGLI/TSGLI.htm

Map of Fisher House Locations
http://fisherhouse.org/aboutUs/7_FHmap.pdf

VA Readjustment Counseling Service (RCS)
www.vetcenter.va.gov, 1-800-905-4675 or 1-866-496-8838. Bereavement
Counseling at 202-273-9116

Sew Much Comfort, adapted clothing for injured military members
www.sewmuchcomfort.org

The Military Severely Injured Center
http://tinyurl.com/2wk4px, 1-888-774-1361

Information About the Medical Evaluation Process
http://tinyurl.com/2ot7na

Tragedy Assistance Program for Survivors (TAPS)
www.taps.org, 1-800-959-TAPS

Gold Star Wives
www.goldstarwives.org/resources-military-family.htm

Society of Military Widows
www.militarywidows.org

Snowball Express
www.snowballexpress.org

Operation Ensuring Christmas
www.opchristmas.org

The Casualty Assistance Office for Each Branch

Branch	Casualty Assistance Office Website
Army	www.armycasualty.army.mil
Air Force	www.afcrossroads.com/casualty/main.cfm#
Navy	www.npc.navy.mil/CommandSupport/CasualtyAssistance
Marine Corps	http://tinyurl.com/2ngyba
Coast Guard	www.uscg.mil/hq/psc/ras/sbp.asp

TRICARE Contact Information

TRICARE Website
www.tricare.mil

CONUS TRICARE Regions and Contact Information

TRICARE Region	Provider	Phone Number	Website
North	HealthNet	1-877-874-2273	www.healthnetfederalservices.com
South	Humana Military	1-800-444-5445	www.humana-military.com
West	TriWest	1-888-874-9378	www.triWest.com

The states covered in each region are shown in Chapter 1 or available at www.tricare.mil

Overseas TRICARE Regions and Contact Information

TRICARE Region	Locations Covered	Phone Number	Website
Europe	Europe, Africa, Middle East	011-49-6302-67-7432	www.tricare.mil/europe
Pacific	Guam, Japan, Korea, Asia, New Zealand, India, Western Pacific remote countries	011-81-6117-43-2036	www.tricare.mil/pacific
Latin America & Canada	Central & South America, the Caribbean Basin, Canada, Puerto Rico, the Virgin Islands	1-706-787-2424	www.tricare.mil/tlac

All phone numbers are as if called from the U.S. Replace the 011 with your international dial code if you are outside the U.S.

Toll-free number for all OCONUS TRICARE Area Offices (calling from within the United States): 1-888-777-8343.

TRICARE Dental Program (United Concordia)
www.tricaredentalprogram.com

Retirement

Transition Assistance Program
www.turbotap.org

Finding a new career
www.taonline.com

Thrift Savings Plan (TSP)
www.tsp.gov

Retirement Pay Calculators
www.defenselink.mil/militarypay/retirement/calc/index.html

TRICARE For Life
www.tricare.mil/mybenefit/home/overview/Plans/ForLife?

TRICARE Retiree Dental Program (TRDP)
www.trdp.org/pro/overview.html

Veterans' Group Life Insurance
www.insurance.va.gov/sgliSite/VGLI/VGLI.htm

Appendix C

Acronyms

AER—Army Emergency Relief

AFAS—Air Force Aid Society

AFSC—Air Force Specialty Code (job type for Air Force)

BAH—Basic Allowance for Housing

BAS—Basic Allowance for Subsistence

CDC—Child Development Center

CDH—Child Development Home (Navy)

CGMA—Coast Guard Mutual Assistance

COLA—Cost of Living Allowance

CONUS—Continental United States

DEERS—Defense Enrollment Eligibility Reporting System

DFAS—Defense Finance and Accounting Service

DITY—Do-It-Yourself Move

DLA—Dislocation Allowance

DoD—Department of Defense

EOS—End of Service (date your spouse leaves the military)

FCC—Family Child Care

FRG—Family Readiness Group

FSGLI—Family of Servicemember Group Life Insurance

HHG—Household Goods

HOR—Home Of Record

IA—Individual Augmentation (type of Navy deployment)

LES—Leave and Earnings Statement

M&IE—Meals and Incidental Expenses

MIHA—Move-In Housing Allowance (overseas only)

MOS—Military Occupation Specialty (job type for Marine Corps and Army)

MTF—Military Treatment Facility (usually base hospital)

MWR—Morale, Welfare, and Recreation

NEC—Navy Enlisted Classification (job type for Navy)

NMCRS—Navy & Marine Corps Relief Society

O-COLA—Overseas Cost Of Living Allowance

OCONUS—Outside Continental United States (includes Alaska and Hawaii)

OHA—Overseas Housing Allowance (like BAH)

OEF—Operation Enduring Freedom

OIF—Operation Iraqi Freedom

OPSEC—Operational Security (keeping information from the enemy)

PCM—Primary Care Manager (your assigned doctor)

PCS—Permanent Change of Station

PDS—Permanent Duty Station

POA—Power Of Attorney

PPO—Personal Property Office

PSD—Personnel Support Detachment

R&R—Rest and Recuperation (time off in the middle of a deployment)

SGLI—Servicemember Group Life Insurance

TAP—Transition Assistance Program

TAPS—Tragedy Assistance Program for Survivors

TDY (or TAD)—Temporary Duty

TLE—Temporary Lodging Expense (CONUS)

TLA—Temporary Lodging Allowance (OCONUS)

TMO—Transportation Management Office

TO—Transportation Office

TSP—Thrift Savings Plan

UA—Unauthorized Absence (also known as AWOL, absent without leave)

UB—Unaccompanied Baggage (overseas shipments only)

VA—Veterans Affairs

VITA—Volunteer Income Tax Assistance

VGLI—Veterans Group Life Insurance

VRO—Vehicle Registration Office

Index